David Torkington's Trilogy
on Prayer comprises

The Hermit
The Prophet
The Mystic

D1295519

In memory of Tony Torkington
Loving Husband, Father and Brother

The Prophet

The Inner Meaning of Prayer

DAVID TORKINGTON

ALBA·HOUSE   NEW·YORK

SOCIETY OF ST. PAUL, 2187 VICTORY BLVD., STATEN ISLAND, NEW YORK 10314

ST PAULS

Library of Congress Cataloging-in-Publication Data

Torkington, David.
    The prophet: the inner meaning of prayer / David Torkington.
        p.   cm.
    Sequel to: The hermit.
    ISBN 0-8189-0851-3
    I. Title.
    PR6070.0657P76   1999
    823'.914 — dc21   98-49631
                                                          CIP

Produced and designed in the United States of America by the
Fathers and Brothers of the Society of St. Paul,
2187 Victory Boulevard, Staten Island, New York 10314,
as part of their communications apostolate.

Published in the United States of America by special arrangement
with Mercier Press, Cork, Ireland.
    ISBN 0-8189-0850-5 — The Hermit
    ISBN 0-8189-0851-3 — The Prophet
    ISBN 0-8189-0852-1 — The Mystic
    ISBN 0-8189-0859-9 — 3-Volume Trilogy on Prayer

© Copyright 1987 Spennithorne Publications

All rights reserved. No part of this publication may be reproduced, stored in
a retrieval system, or transmitted in any form or by any means without the
prior written permission of the publisher, nor be otherwise circulated in
any form of binding or cover other than that in which it is published and
without a similar condition being imposed on the subsequent purchase.

Printing Information:

Current Printing - first digit   1   2   3   4   5   6   7   8   9   10

Year of Current Printing - first year shown

1999   2000   2001   2002   2003   2004   2005   2006   2007

1

I felt as if I'd been kneed in the stomach from the inside.

I flung the newspaper to the ground and buried my head in my hands, stunned by the shattering news that I had just read.

Eventually I leaned forward, picked the paper off the ground and re-read the short paragraph headed "Fisherman Lost at Sea." I read it over and over, hoping that it was all some terrible mistake, but it wasn't. The words remained exactly the same.

A local Hebridean fisherman, known as Peter Calvay, was presumed lost at sea after a three day air and sea search by local rescue teams, reinforced by R.A.F. helicopters and a naval supply vessel en route for Icelandic waters.

I slumped back into my chair, almost physically paralyzed by the terrible news, but all sorts of things were happening in my head. Only a short time ago I had been introduced to Peter Calvay by a chance meeting with one of his correspondents at a local retreat center. I had made a special journey out to his island home to seek the help I needed to save me from a spiritual disaster that was threatening to overtake me.

I was not disappointed — it turned out that he was not only a true hermit, but a mystic too who totally changed the direction of my life not just by what he said, but by what he was.

I had written to him only a few weeks before from my new home in Birmingham to arrange a further meeting in the early Autumn and now this!

I don't know how long I slouched in the chair staring vacantly into space, but gradually from a kaleidoscope of images and ideas that flashed and flickered in my mind a single shoddy thought took hold of me. What am I to do now? What am I to do now?

Suddenly, I pulled myself together and got to my feet, shaken back into reality by my own selfish reaction to the tragedy of Peter's death.

"Next, please," said the receptionist, opening the door into the dentist's surgery. "It's Father Robertson, I think." She looked at me rather apprehensively.

I was still standing in the middle of the floor, fists clenched, lips tightly pursed together, eyes flaming with anger at my own selfishness.

"There's nothing to be afraid of," she said, trying to force a reassuring smile.

"I'm not afraid of anything," I replied rather ridiculously as I stormed past her and the waiting dentist, and sat down in the chair.

He seemed rather perplexed and somewhat embarrassed by the odd little scene that had just taken place, and began to cover his confusion by rapidly sticking all sorts of surgical instruments into my mouth.

It was the most painful session I have ever had to endure at the dentist. I couldn't relax, and my tension communicated itself to the dentist with painful consequences for my poor mouth.

As soon as the dentist had filled two large molars, I rushed out into the waiting-room without even pausing to thank him, and picked up the paper once more.

"Good gracious, no!" I said to myself as I looked at its date. It was almost a month old.

"May I have this paper?" I said to the receptionist.

"Of course," she replied. "But it will be a few days old, I'm afraid."

"Days? You mean weeks, don't you?" I shouted rudely as I rushed out of the waiting-room.

As soon as I got home I rang up Father James, the parish priest of Northbay, Barra, where Peter had his island hermitage.

He tried to tell me all that had happened but it was almost impossible to make head or tail of what he said between the crackles on the line. I just about gathered that Peter had set off for the island of Calvay after giving some talk or other, but he never arrived, and there had been no trace of him since.

The funeral had taken place a week later, minus the body, which was presumed lost at sea.

"It was a terrible shock to all of us," he said.

"Look, Father," I shouted down the line. "I'm coming out as soon as I can manage it. Can you find me a bed for a few nights?"

"By all means," he replied. "Come as soon as you like."

It took some arranging because the small Island plane for Barra was fully booked for the next three weeks, so I took the train to Oban and sailed to Castlebay, the capital of the island.

Father Murdoch, a friend of Father James, waited to meet me at the boat which got in at one o'clock in the morning. He insisted on giving me what he called "a wee dram" before I went to bed.

For those unfamiliar with the Scottish language, the word "wee" means small or little when applied to anything bar the local wine.

Father Murdoch's "wee dram" assured me of a good night's sleep that lasted until the middle of the next day!

He told me that Father James (the priests are usually referred to by their first names in the Isles) wouldn't be in until late afternoon, so he insisted that I stayed for lunch during which he told me more about the circumstances surrounding Peter's death.

It appeared that Father Murdoch had decided to have a Mission for his parish, and each evening he had asked Peter to give a series of talks on Christian spirituality to a group of religious Sisters, who worked on the islands. For the first time Peter had accepted such an invitation.

After his first talk on the Monday evening, Peter had stayed the night at the presbytery and set off posthaste at first light. Nobody but a local fisherman saw him cast off for Calvay at about five in the morning. It would have been about fourteen miles to Calvay, and he should have made it in two to three hours. However, he didn't arrive and nobody had seen him since, in spite of an intensive air and sea search that went on for several days.

It was about five o'clock when Father Murdoch dropped me off at the presbytery in Northbay. He didn't come in, as he had to get back for an evening Mass at six o'clock. Father James was delighted to see me though it was quite obvious that Peter's death had shaken him and, as I found out later, he had been far closer to Peter than I had ever known.

We didn't talk much about Peter until after dinner. He then related the story for me once more adding a few relevant details that Father Murdoch had not mentioned. The strange thing was that the sea had been perfectly calm on the morning that Peter had disappeared, and in fact there hadn't been any rough seas in the area since. However, Father James explained that incidents of this sort were not uncommon among fishermen. Almost every fishing community has its strange tales of men and boats that are mysteriously lost at sea without any natural explanation. Only a few years previously a trawler from the mainland had disappeared without any trace whatsoever while fishing in the North Sea. The strange thing was that the Captain's old grandmother, who was supposed to have the gift of second sight, had had some sort of premonition, and had pleaded with her grandson on the quay not to go, but he only laughed, and told her to go home and knit the sweater she had promised to give him for Christmas. He said he'd be home with a bumper catch before she could finish it.

She was sitting in her daughter's kitchen, when she suddenly threw her knitting to the ground and said that the ship had been sunk and the whole crew lost. Nobody would believe her at the time in spite of her reputation, but she was right. The funny thing is that when Canon MacFee, the local parish priest, asked for prayers for Peter only two weeks ago, old Granny MacDonald said they wouldn't be necessary because Peter was alive and well in hospital.

"How incredible," I said. "Do you think she could possibly be right?"

Father James momentarily raised his eyebrows without saying anything as if to say, "Who knows" but after a pause he said, "I'm afraid not. The evidence is quite clear. Every hospital north of Fleetwood has been contacted as well as in Northern Ireland, but none of them has any record of admitting anybody who could possibly be Peter. The Army from the rocket range on South Uist and the Navy joined forces to make a thorough search of the whole area, but there was no sign of Peter or his little boat."

Father James gazed thoughtfully at the floor for a few moments. "Now look, Father," he said, "I'm glad you've come out here because there is something I would like to ask you to do for me."

"But of course," I said. "I would be delighted to do anything I can for you."

"Now how are you fixed for time?"

"Well, I have arranged to stay for a week's holiday if that's all right with you. I will take the plane back to Birmingham next Wednesday."

"Oh dear, I don't want to spoil your holiday," said Father James. "Please forget all about it."

"No, not at all," I protested. "What is it you want me to do for you? I can always say no."

"Well, the position is this. Somebody will have to go through Peter's things: all his personal effects, his letters, and whatever else he has got in his little cottage. I know he did an awful lot of writing. You are the only priest he has ever spoken to at any length, and I know he used to write to you a lot so you're probably more on his wave length than me. Anyway, I'm just no good at that sort of thing."

"I would be absolutely delighted. In fact, if you can take me over tomorrow I'll get started right away. But what sort of state is the house in?" I asked.

"Oh, don't worry about that. Peter was no masochist, I can

assure you of that. You'll find it warm and cosy and the bed is almost new."

"I'm pleased to hear it," I said. "I've flirted with most 'isms' in my time, but I've not so much as made a pass at asceticism. I don't think we are constitutionally compatible. By the way, how on earth did Peter manage to build a cottage out there?" I asked. "How did he transport all the bricks, and other building materials?"

"Most of them were there already," said Father James.

"Already there? How do you mean?"

"Well, a small Hebridean black-house was built on the island in the late 1830's, but it was destroyed in the winter of 1851. The foundations were left and two walls were still standing when I took Peter out to see it some fifteen years ago.

"Destroyed by what?"

"Destroyed by whom, you should have said," said Father James, suddenly looking serious.

"What would anybody want to pull it down for?"

"You may well ask," said Father James tersely, as if he had been personally involved in the incident himself, and was trying to hold back a wave of pent up emotion.

I knew there was a story to be told, and he would tell me, but I didn't know how to ask him to proceed without seeming to pry into what was obviously a matter that touched him deeply.

"They must have been hard times," I said.

"They were terrible times," he said. "Times that we can never forget."

"Oh, do you mean the Highland clearances?" I said, suddenly remembering I had read a book on the subject during my last visit.

"I do indeed," he said.

"I suppose the Highlanders must still feel very bitter towards the English for what they did," I said, feeling that it must have been the English who were to blame, as it had been in Ireland.

"It wasn't the English," said Father James. "It was our own chiefs with their lust for money and their sheep, who betrayed us."

"I'm afraid I should know, but I fear my knowledge of those times is rather hazy," I admitted. "How did it all come about?"

"It's a long story," he said, "but the short of it is this. In the old days a chief was a chief. It was people that came first, not cattle. The chief may sometimes have been a tyrant, he might have had the power of life and death over his clansmen, but for all that he was as often as not a protector too, and in his own way a father to his people. After the Jacobite rebellion in 1745 things gradually began to change as the old chiefs died out. The English stripped the chieftains of their authority. They no longer had the power of 'gallows and pit,' and as their powers waned, so did their paternal interest and protection. They were now no longer warrior chiefs but landowners. The younger chiefs were seduced by the sophistication and soft living of the southerners. They had to have fine houses in Edinburgh or even London. They married wives from the lowlands or England, who wanted more than stone walls to live in, and home-spun cloth on their backs. They wanted fine clothes, carriages, and fashionable homes in which to entertain their friends.

"The Highland chief didn't want anyone to treat him with disdain, because he came from what was thought to be the barren and barbarous North. Nor did he want them to think he was their inferior in taste or culture. He wanted to send his sons to school in England, and buy coveted commissions for them in the most prestigious regiments. All this needed money. Money, money and more money. The problem was where to get it from. His faithful clansmen might follow him to hell and back with a broad-sword in their hands, they made the best and bravest of warriors, but they made poor tenants, as they pitifully tried to eke out a living from their poor infertile tracts of land.

"Then a new invader began to make incursions into the far North. An invader with four feet, who was destined to rob the clansmen of their ancestral homes."

"Sheep," I said.

"Aye! Sheep. Cheviots — a new breed from the south that

7

could live through the severest winter and produce three and four times the amount of wool and meat than their Highland cousins. This was how the clearances started. It was not the English, but the chiefs, who were for the most part absentee landlords, who cared less and less for their own clansmen, and more and more for the money they could get out of their more profitable sheep. Thousands upon thousands of men, women and children had their houses literally burnt over their heads if they didn't get out quickly enough. Many of them wandered into the slums of Glasgow, or other major cities. Many more were unceremoniously put aboard ships, some manacled like slaves, bound for North America, Canada or Australia."

"But that's terrible," I said. "What about the law?"

"Oh, yes, there was the law, but the law was on the side of the chiefs. It was the chiefs who actually owned the land; the rest were only tenants with short leases lasting no more than a year. It was the law that drove them out of their homes. It was the law that herded them on to the overcrowded transporters, where many of them died of starvation if they escaped the plague or the pox."

"But that was terrible," I said.

"It was second only to the slave trade in its inhuman barbarity," said Father James bitterly. "Peter's cottage was built by an Islander, who was transported to make room for sheep." He paused momentarily. "You see, the Islanders' turn came almost at the end of the clearances. Barra belonged to a notorious Colonel Gordon, who had once thought of selling the island as a penal colony but decided to populate it with sheep instead. The poor men of Barra were left to the mercies of an officious officer called Beatson, but he had no mercy on them. Angus MacNeil built his house on Calvay some fourteen years before, thinking that if the clearances were to come to the Isles he would be safe and sound, but he wasn't. It was Beatson himself who had a boat lowered from a passing transporter when he spied Angus's cottage, and together with half a dozen constables he landed on Calvay. It was a cold winter's day on the fourth of December, 1851.

"When Angus saw them coming, he with his wife and two children barricaded themselves inside their little house, but it did no good. The constables battered down the door and dragged them out. Angus was a champion wrestler — a man of enormous strength — but even he was no match for six men of the law bearing heavy truncheons. He fought bravely but they felled him to the ground with their weapons in front of his wife and children. They handcuffed him and dragged him off to the boat then set fire to the house. It was then that Morag, his wife, let out a terrible scream and rushed into the house where her own mother lay in her sick-bed. The blankets that she was wrapped in were on fire when two of the constables dragged her out.

"Do you know what those devils did next?" said Father James, staring at me with eyes blazing all afire. "They clubbed the demented Morag to the ground, and carried her senseless with her children to the waiting boat, leaving the poor sick granny to fend for herself, to forage for food and shelter in the ashes of her own home. And all this in front of two wee girls of eight and eleven years of age." He paused for a moment, shaking his head at the hideous cruelty of the whole episode.

"And what happened to the old granny?" I said.

"Well, the smoke from the cottage was seen from the mainland, but nobody dared to come near the island until the next day for fear they, too, might be carried off by the constables. The next morning a group of fishermen sailed over from Northbay, and found the poor old granny there. She had died of exposure during the night."

"It just doesn't seem possible," I said. "How did you come to hear the whole story?"

"Because that eleven-year-old-girl was my grandmother," said Father James. His voice was shaking with emotion. "I heard the whole story from her own lips in 1922 when she was eighty-two. She died in 1930 at the age of ninety."

"Good God!" I gasped.

Somehow the close personal link with those terrible events

seemed to heighten the horror of the atrocities and telescoped the intervening years in such a way that it seemed as if it had happened only yesterday.

I looked at Father James as I'd never looked at him before. He'd hardly been a person to me until now. He'd only been a means of contact with Peter, but in those brief moments I'd met him for the first time.

He was looking impassively out to sea through the open window, mulling over the brutal injustice meted out to his forebears, feeling deep down the mixed emotions that swelled up from within. His great-grandfather would have been proud of him, a magnificent mountain of a man, still powerful in every way though he would be in his mid-sixties by now. I could imagine him in his youth, stripped to vest and kilt, tossing the caber four feet or more beyond his fellows. I could see him at Culloden wielding a claymore like a warrior from the Waverley novels, scything down half a handful of red-coated penguins with a gigantic swish of his blade. But that was only the man of my momentary imagination; the man I saw before me was still big, big in every way. He was a man who had been mellowed by the passing years; weather-worn, rounded and softened, with the experience of sharing the heartache and the thousand natural shocks of his own folk, for whom he was now the only laird they knew. He was one of those rare men, Peter had told me, who always seemed to have time for everyone whoever they were. He was always there whenever there was a crisis or a cross to be borne; always there at the major cross-roads in the lives of the only highland sheep that mattered to him.

"Sorry about that outburst," said Father James, conscious that his understandable emotions had got the better of him.

"Not at all," I said. "You've every right to be angry. I'm angry myself that such a dreadful thing could happen; that human beings could possibly treat one another in such an inhuman way."

"Well," said Father James, "Let's say no more about it. I'll show you to your bed."

He stalked up the stairway, showed me to my room and was gone before I knew what had happened. It was quite evident that he was on the verge of tears, and he had to act quickly to avoid making a fool of himself in front of a visitor.

I walked over to the window and looked across the sea to Calvay, and then I looked down to the small jetty at the back of the presbytery. It was early June and although it had passed ten o'clock it was still quite light. My mind went back to my last visit to Barra eighteen months before when I had met Peter for the first time and learned so much from him about the spiritual life. It just didn't seem possible that he was dead. For the first time I began to feel sorry for Peter himself, for his tragic death, and for the many people who, like myself, had depended upon him for spiritual help and direction. Still, maybe I could be of some help, I mused as I got into bed, and began to dream about what I would be able to do. After all, he wrote to dozens of people from all over the world, and I knew he always kept copies of his letters. Maybe he had written down his own spiritual reflections.

I began to imagine how I could edit and possibly publish his spiritual teaching on prayer and the spiritual life, and even bathe a little in his reflected glory. My self-indulgent imaginings were suddenly interrupted as Father James first knocked, and then came into the room with half a tumbler full of neat malt whisky in his hand.

"I'm sorry. I got so carried away that I forgot to give you a wee dram to welcome you back to Barra." He smiled. He was quite composed now, and fully in control of himself, but he didn't stay. "Slánte," he said in Gaelic, as he was closing the door. "Goodnight and God bless. Have a good sleep. There's a lot of work waiting for you tomorrow on Calvay."

I was awakened by **2** strange sounds and shuffles from the kitchen, which I discovered was directly beneath my bedroom. I vaguely remembered hearing someone turning on a tap and filling a kettle full of water. I glanced at my watch. It was almost a quarter to eight. So what, I thought, as I turned over, and drifted back into semi-slumber land.

Some time later I was half conscious of the kitchen door opening. Someone was taking the lid off a dust-bin in the yard beneath my window. It must have been the housekeeper, because I heard Father James shouting to her from inside.

"I'm just taking Father Robertson a cup of tea."

It took between five and ten seconds before the full implication of his words burst into my consciousness with devastating effect.

Before you could say "Jack," never mind "Robinson," I was out of my bed confronting the object that threatened to humiliate me, if I didn't move fast. Half a tumbler full of neat malt whisky stood on my bedside table innocently unaware of the embarrassing predicament that it had put me in. Something simply had to be done to save face. I knew I couldn't possibly drink it first thing in the morning without disastrous consequences to my constitution.

In a flash I picked up the glass and rushed over to the door, but it was too late to make it to the bathroom. I could hear Father James; he was almost at the top of the stairs. If necessity is the mother of invention then impending humiliation is the father of inspirational genius. At least, it was for me that morning. In less than one shake of a lamb's tail I was back in bed, looking half asleep as Father James tapped on the door and came in to place a cup of tea on my bedside table.

"Well now," he said. "Could you eat a hearty breakfast? Eggs and bacon, and all the trimmings?"

"Indeed I could," I said enthusiastically as I sat up in bed.

"Good man," he replied, picking up the empty tumbler and examining it with approval. "I always say that a man who can eat a hearty breakfast is a man who can hold his drink."

I smiled modestly as if I'd just been complimented by the village elder for passing the prescribed test of my manhood.

He opened the curtains for me, and nearly knocked a large gangly geranium off the chest of drawers in the process.

"Confound it!" he said, as he managed to prevent the pot from falling to the ground.

"I see you've been watering it for me," he said, as he looked at the liquid that had collected in the saucer beneath the pot!

"Yes," I said hurriedly. "I'm a keen gardener."

"Well, let's hope you've got green fingers. It's not flowered for over eighteen months." He opened the door. "Breakfast will be ready in about fifteen minutes." The door closed.

I could breathe again. Let's hope I've not done any permanent damage, I thought. But after all, if the average Scotsman can drink more than five gallons of whisky a year, a 'wee dram' would hardly do an over-sized geranium any harm, at least once in its lifetime.

"I've got to go to Castlebay to get a few provisions for you," said Father James as soon as we had finished breakfast. "And a couple of canisters of Calor gas for you to take over to the island. I'll be back in an hour or two. Meanwhile, perhaps you'd like to read these — they are six autobiographical essays that Peter wrote charting his own spiritual odyssey.

"They were never intended for publication, or anything like that — I think he must have written them when I asked him to give six talks to religious Sisters, so that he would have some written material as a point of reference. There is in fact a lot of personal material in them that was obviously never intended for use in the talks, which he included for his own purposes. I think you'll find them fascinating reading, I know I did."

As soon as Father James left I sat down to read the first typescript that was entitled:

FROM LONDON TO DUBLIN

'Towards the end of my first year at teachers' training college I went with my fellow students at Strawberry Hill, to a moral leadership course in London. It was run by a group of priests from various congregations.

'Before splitting us up into groups the priest in charge explained that Jesus was the King of all virtues. He was the embodiment of all true virtue. If we wanted to imitate Him we must first study Him, and His exemplary dealings with others.

'In order to do this we were taught how to meditate, or to "contemplate" as the priest called the exercise, in which we had to picture Gospel scenes using our imagination wherever possible to home in on the exemplary behavior of Jesus.

'Then the members of the groups would discuss the virtues that they had discovered and list them in order of priority so that by the end of the course we had produced a sort of league table of all the most important virtues.

'"Now," said the priest at the end of the course, "you can see clearly where you are going. If you want to become a Christ-like person you must try to acquire the virtues that we have discovered together." As a sort of afterthought he said, "Oh, any questions or queries?"

'The priest didn't really expect a question. In those days people didn't question much anyway, and Father had run many of these courses. The formula had been well tried, the outcome predictable, even if the participants thought otherwise. So Father was obviously a little surprised when one of the students stood up. The priest looked slightly apprehensive but only slightly. After all, this would most likely be a vote of thanks, but it wasn't.

"'Well, Father," said the young man, "I would like to thank you, and the other priests for all that you have done to try to make this course a success. However, I can only speak for myself when I say that I have found the course very disappointing. You see, even if I agreed with your approach, which I am afraid I don't, I still don't see the point of the course. In general we can all see more or less how we ought to behave if we want to become Christ-like people — but that's not our main problem. Our main moral problem is that we can't do it. It's the same dilemma that St. Paul found himself in. He could see how he ought to have behaved but he didn't have the inner power and strength to do it.

"'Surely this is the 64,000 dollar question? Where do we go to, or rather to whom do we go, to receive the inner power and strength to make us into Christ-like people? It is a question that this course doesn't even attempt to answer."

'There was something a little too patronizing about the way the priest nodded his head as the young man spoke. Something a little too glib about the way he replied almost before the last syllable was out of his mouth.

"'May I suggest that you come to our follow-up course entitled 'Tools of the Trade,'" he said, "when we attempt to show how to acquire the self-same virtues that we have been discerning in the life of Christ this weekend. And secondly, may I emphasize that the Grace of God will always be necessary, if we are going to generate any authentic Christian virtue."

'The young man stood up again. He was obviously quite worked up, but was well able to speak for himself.

"'I followed the course 'Tools of the Trade' last year, Father," he said. "This is why I am concerned with the whole approach used in these moral leadership courses. It only pays lip service to the action of God's grace in the spiritual life, while placing all the practical emphasis on human man-made methods and techniques, as the prime way to attain the virtues that lead to full Christian maturity. I am not a Scripture scholar or a theologian, Father, but

I do have a doctorate in philosophy — Greek philosophy to be more precise, and this enables me to see that these courses have as much, if not more, in common with Greek moralism than with a Christian mysticism that is surely at the very heart of the Gospel.

"'Forgive me for being so blunt, but these courses do not reflect the true spirit of the Gospels at all but rather the spirit of the Renaissance.

"'Please can we have the Gospel in future, not a pagan moralism thinly disguised as Christianity?'"

'The young man spoke with such authority and confidence that the priest began to wilt visibly as he expanded and pressed home the point he was making. We were all disappointed when the bell for night prayer suddenly ended what was beginning to develop into a fascinating discussion. All, that is, save the priest who had already realized that he had more than the usual raw and rebellious youth to deal with.

'All of us had been satisfied with the course that had just ended, at least until Julian, for that was the young philosopher's name, had given us all pause for thought. He had been able to verbalize for me in such a clear and coherent way vague misgivings that were only just beginning to be formed in the back of my mind.

'Julian sat next to me on the coach journey back to college and I had a fascinating conversation with him. He explained to me how, when Europe was in her early teens, she'd had a love affair with the classical world of Greece and Rome, that had inspired her to re-design every aspect of her life and culture after the ideal world that she thought she had discovered in the past. This new movement was called a re-birth or a Renaissance. While the writers, poets and the artists of the day were being totally dominated by the influence of their classical Greek and Roman forebears, the thinkers, the intellectuals and the philosophers were influenced in the same way by the great Socrates, the Greek philosophical genius who became the undisputed guru of the new movement whose exemplary moral teaching was almost universally applauded and accepted.

'Although Socrates argued to the existence of God, he couldn't argue, by reason alone, to a God who had any interest in Man whatsoever. Man could only therefore better himself by the moral behavior that he learned for himself and then attained by his own unaided human endeavor. That's what is meant by a "moralism." So you see, the great credo of the Renaissance was not "I believe in God," but "I believe in Man," and in how he can change himself, and the world he lives in, by his own efforts alone.

'It was primarily to counteract his incredible influence that Christianity began to present Jesus as their Socrates, an even greater philosopher, whose moral teaching was even loftier than his Greek counterpart. They were so successful that to this day many still misinterpret and misrepresent Jesus and the message He came to bring. He is not primarily a moral philosopher who has come to detail the way in which we are to love God and our neighbor, but a mystic who has come to give us the power to do it. He does this by showing us by the example of His own life how to expose ourselves to the inner power and strength that alone will enable us to love God perfectly and to love our neighbor, as God loves us.

'True Christian virtue is but the outward human expression of the divine life working from within.

'I had never looked at the Gospel in that way before. Julian's clear and incisive reasoning was already leading me into my first real conversion experience. A conversion to the religion that I had been brought up and educated in, but which I had never really fully understood before.

'"Yes, I see what you mean, Julian," I said. "But what is the next practical step for me to take because I do genuinely want to imitate Jesus Christ?"

'Julian's answer came without any hesitation.

'"By imitating Jesus from the inside. By doing what Jesus Himself did to allow His weak human nature to be possessed progressively by the life and the love of His Father. Once filled by the same life that animated Him, then genuine Christ-like behavior follows as a matter of course."

'I lay awake for hours that night thinking over everything Julian had said. When I finally got up my mind was made up. If I was really serious about imitating Jesus, I simply had to have an environment in which to expose myself to the self-same life and light that was the principle of all He said and did. Only in this way could I really follow Him.

'I saw clearly that morning, more clearly than I had ever seen before, that prayer was merely the word used by Christian tradition to describe the way we go about radically exposing ourselves to the self-same Spirit that progressively penetrated the heart and mind of Jesus. This is why prayer was so important in the life of Jesus Himself, and of all those who have followed Him throughout the ages. This is why they all sought out solitude with such regularity. This is why they all had such a desperate need for an environment in which to be alone before God, so that the very life of God Himself, the Holy Spirit, could in some measure bring about the incarnation again in them, so that Christ could be present in and through them, to all.

'There and then I made my decision. I would leave the training college and become a religious. It seemed the logical thing to do.

'The Father Provincial readily accepted me and I was sent to the novitiate in Dublin that very September. However, he made it clear that I might never be ordained a priest because of my handicap. One leg was six inches shorter than the other as a result of polio, which struck me down at the age of six, and forced me to wear an iron caliper and use a stick ever since. I couldn't have cared less. I wanted to be a religious; to be more accurate I wanted God, and the time to expose myself to the life that I knew would alone enable me to become a Christ-like person.

'The experience I had had on the moral leadership course and my conversation with Julian led me to choose one of the older

Orders whose traditions pre-dated the Renaissance, so that I would be grounded in an authentic Christian spirituality, free from the influence of the pagan moralism that had already had such an influence on my Christian formation.

'I was still rather naive for I had not yet realized that the spirituality of both the newer and the older Orders had all been deeply influenced by the Renaissance, and therefore by a humanism that owed as much if not more to Socrates, the philosopher of Athens, than to Jesus Christ, the prophet of Nazareth.

'There were sixteen novices who stood up the first time the Novice Master came into the recreation room to address us. I'll never forget his first words.

'"My dear novices, I am going to break you and remold you."

'In the subsequent weeks he explained how original sin had molded us all into moral monstrosities, and how with his help we would have to be broken and re-set in the image and likeness of Jesus Christ.

'The Novice Master would help us to discern the particular faults and failings that distorted each of us, with a little help from the other novices, who were encouraged to discard what he called their "school-boy scruples," and inform him of the misdemeanors of the others.

'Prayer was primarily a time for what was called "contemplation" in which we were taught to re-create Gospel scenes in our minds, and whenever possible with our imaginations too so that we could study the man we had been called upon to follow. The feeling of "déjà vu" was confirmed when he explained that Christ was the King of all virtue, in whom alone we would find the virtues that we must learn to acquire for ourselves. As the vices of the "Old Man" were removed, then the virtues of the "New Man" would be put in their place.

'Certain forms of mortification like the discipline, the clamp and other ascetical practices were suggested, or even imposed to help the "Old Man" die a little more quickly. Humiliation was the favorite device employed by the Novice Master, because it was in his opinion the quickest and straightest road to humility, the foundation of all the virtues.

'You may well say, "Thank God that the old-fashioned approach is dead and buried," but it isn't entirely. Don't be deceived. The old emphasis on the study of the classics may have all but disappeared from secular education, just as the crude implementation of a "Christian stoicism" may have disappeared from religious education, but the pernicious humanism, the "man can make himself perfect" mentality that is at its very heart still persists. The only difference today is that the methods have changed, as the latest pop-psychology is now the "panacea," to do what the old methods failed to achieve.

'In spite of the dreadful regime that I had to endure in the novitiate, I nevertheless persevered for eleven months before leaving, mainly because despite everything else we did have a minimum of three hours of silence and solitude each day. I used to love this, and used every minute of it for the prayer that I saw so clearly was the only way to allow the power of God in, to do to death the "Old Man" in me and bring to birth the New.

'This conviction was reinforced by the spiritual reading that clearly demonstrated this truth in the lives of the saints, and the other great spiritual masters from the past. I could not get over the fact that in the very place that should be its bastion, prayer was simply misunderstood, neglected or reduced to saying prayers.

'I went back to teachers' training college to continue my studies, but I was a different person for something strange had happened to me in the novitiate which was totally to change my life, but it took me years to realize the full significance of what had happened.

'After eight months the highly charged and emotional prayer that I was beginning to believe was a sign that I was about to reach the top of Mt. Tabor suddenly disappeared, literally over-night, nor did it return in the following months though I did everything to retrieve what I had lost. I sought every sort of advice that was available to me, but I could find no one who could explain my sudden change of fortune. Even a brilliant theologian who came from our house of studies to give us a course on Christology was of little or no help, though he did counsel perseverance and mistrust of the feelings, that can easily be a misleading measure of spiritual success.

'When I asked him about some of the classical mystical authors that I was reading in the hope that they would explain my predicament, he admitted with a humility that incensed rather than inspired me that he had no knowledge whatsoever about mystical theology.

'How on earth can a theologian know all about God and how God operates among men without any experiential knowledge of His action? Mystical theology is only the word used to describe the psychological implications of experiencing the action of God as His Spirit invades our inmost being to fashion us into Christ-like human beings.

'I was dumbfounded that a man so learned in what was called the "new theology" only understood his subject like an outsider with the cold intellectual knowledge of a classical scholar. I was reading *The Desert Fathers* at the time and the words of Evagrius Ponticus rang in my ears. *"A theologian is a man of prayer, and a man of prayer is a theologian."*

'While I continued to study at Strawberry Hill I still felt drawn to prayer and regularly gave time in the evenings for the solitude that I desired, but I seemed to be getting nowhere, and although I still persevered, I simply didn't know what to do.

'I began to search far and wide for someone to help me but I searched in vain. I began to think that there was something wrong with me, and the thought occurred to me that it might be more fruitful to seek out the help of a psychiatrist rather than the help of a priest. Then Fate stepped in, and led me to the man who understood, not just me but the whole journey that my heart was already set upon.

'It meant traveling to a distant country with a mountain that had been made holy by centuries of hermits and monks, who had claimed it as their spiritual home. I had heard about it before; I had read about it many times in spiritual books, but I had never dared to imagine, even in my wildest dreams, that one day I'd find myself a pilgrim on the sanctified slopes of Mount Athos.'

Father James would be away for at least another hour and I simply couldn't wait to read the next typescript. It was entitled:

FROM PARIS TO MOUNT ATHOS

'When I'd completed **3** my studies at Strawberry Hill I went to study modern languages at the Sorbonne in Paris, and was delighted to find that my new roommate was a Russian called Boris, an Orthodox Christian, totally committed to the same journey that I had embarked upon myself.

'It was at Easter of that first year that he talked me into going with him to Mount Athos to meet the monk who would become his full-time spiritual director, as soon as he had completed his studies.

'The story of our journey across Europe would merit a book of its own, but I don't want to delay unnecessarily to tell you about what was, for me, the spiritual adventure of a lifetime.

'Father Dimitrius was a Russian monk who had spent many years steeping himself in the spirituality of the desert. It had already formed him into a man of great spiritual depth and wisdom, that set him apart as a holy man to whom all the other monks would turn for knowledge of the mystic way in which he had become a recognized master.

'Boris spent many hours with him while I explored the surrounding countryside and the many ancient monasteries that sprawled over the sacred mountain. My patience was finally rewarded when Boris said that Father Dimitrius would see me, and that he would come in to translate for me, for my Russian was still far from perfect although it soon became almost fluent with Boris's help.

'I don't know who was more dumbfounded, Boris or myself,

when Father Dimitrius turned to me and spoke in impeccable English. He was a remarkable man, tall, elegant and refined, looking for all the world like an English country gentleman dressed in the garb of a Greek Orthodox monk, but penetrated through and through with the wisdom of the East, that permeated everything that he said and did. It turned out that he was a White Russian who'd had to flee from his homeland during the Revolution when he was only a small boy and had been brought up in a little village near Stowmarket in Suffolk, and educated at an English public school.

'I was simply delighted because I hated the idea of conversing with him through an interpreter. Even though Boris was already a good friend, I didn't feel like baring my soul before him. Father Dimitrius understood my predicament completely with all the ease of a master of mathematics listening to the difficulties of a young student grappling with fractions for the first time.

'The sudden change in my prayer life, far from being a sign of spiritual back-sliding or some psychological abnormality, was a sign that I was totally normal. "It happens," he said, " to everyone who takes prayer seriously and gives consistent daily time to what is the most important exercise in the spiritual journey."

'Although he emphasized that it was normal, he nevertheless made it quite clear that it was a special grace of God for which I must be thankful for the rest of my life. He explained how in Christian spirituality the desert is not so much a physical place, but rather an inner state of mind and heart, where God teaches the beginner the most profound secrets of the spiritual way.

'A person is exposed, laid bare in the desert. There they experience their fundamental weakness; they experience that they can do nothing without God, not even pray. The person led into the desert experiences a burning thirst for a closer union with God, but they are so beset with the devil from within, that their most earnest desire is repeatedly frustrated by a thousand and one distractions and temptations, that rise up from the nether regions of their own unpurified personality.

"'You have already been led to the threshold of the desert. Thank God for it," said Father Dimitrius, "for when God leads a person to the edge of the desert, it is the most important moment in the spiritual life. It is unfortunately the great scandal of religious life today that so few people know how to journey on, because so few have traveled before them into the only place where true sanctity is learned.

"'In the desert a person is progressively made more and more aware of their utter weakness, and total dependence upon God to Whom they finally turn and surrender, because frankly there is no one else to turn to, and nowhere else to go.

"'The best translation of the first of the Beatitudes is not 'Blessed are the poor in spirit,' but rather 'Blessed are they who know their need of God.' The real quality of conversion depends on the true knowledge we have of our need of Him, and that knowledge which is true wisdom is learned in the desert, when our need of God is exposed and laid bare as never before.

"'This conversion involves the whole person, to the very marrow of their being, and is far more profound than the emotional conversion of the beginner.

"'If you will bear with me, my friend," said Father Dimitrius, "I would like to tell you a story, a long story of how, when I was in the same predicament as you, I sought out help from a holy monk who taught me the lesson of a lifetime. He taught me the inner meaning of true Christian prayer in a way that I could never forget, and in a way that has sustained me throughout the years.

"'Like you, I was full of enthusiasm when I first began the spiritual journey. Prayer was easy. I loved to linger over the Sacred Scriptures; to pore over the passages that moved me most. One morning when I settled down to the prayer time that had become my greatest joy, everything left me; all feeling of fervor that once meant so much to me suddenly disappeared and the days went by without my initial joy in prayer returning. I had all the fears that you have; all the misgivings that you experience, as everybody has at this particular point in the spiritual journey.

"'However, I was luckier than most because I had been assigned to a great spiritual master. Brother Potentius, the pilgrim, smiled when I explained my plight, and said it was time we made a pilgrimage together to the land of the Lord, to learn there the true meaning of prayer. He was a massive man, a Cossack cavalry officer before he became a monk — a man of few words but of great spiritual wisdom that he hoarded like a miser in his mind. But once sure of a disciple, he would give all that he had received, with a generosity that was limited only by the capacity of the receiver. His huge head was a riot of thick black hair, that so covered his face that only his eyes stood out to search the soul of anyone brave enough to face them. Although he was over seventy when we set off for Palestine I was hard put to it to keep pace with his mighty strides. We arrived at the famous monastery of Marsab shortly before the beginning of Lent, and then we made our way barefoot to the sacred mountain of Temptation, where the Lord had learned the lesson that I still had to learn.

"'We stayed there for almost the whole of Lent, in the holy monastery that is built into the side of the rock face only a matter of meters from the summit. Each day I had to spend hours in prayer on top of the mountain, and I got more and more depressed, because I was going nowhere but backwards. I simply couldn't pray. The spiritual desolation that had prompted me to go to Brother Potentius in the first place got worse and worse with each passing day. In the end I swallowed my pride, and went to see him, and admitted that even this holy place had not helped me to return to true prayer.

"'He said, 'I have purposely sent you to pray upon the holy mountain top where the Savior came to pray, so that you could experience what He experienced, and come to learn the true meaning of prayer.

"''After he has been spoiled and pampered like a child in the prayer of first beginnings, God leads the spiritual adolescent into the desert with His own Son. Here he learns to become an adult by engaging in spiritual combat with the Evil One, which is the very heart and soul of authentic Christian prayer.

""Because Jesus had already experienced the weak human nature that He chose to enter into, He knew that without the sustained help and strength of His Father He would never be able to withstand the gates of hell, that would be opened against Him.

""This is why He went into the desert in the first place, because He knew and experienced His need of the Father. There He came to see, and to understand, that the help and strength He needed from the Father was actually given in the context of a combat with the power of evil, who tried everything to turn Him away from the only One who could sustain Him.

""True prayer is a relentless battle against the Evil One who assails us, most of all in prayer beyond the first beginnings, when terrible distractions and temptations from our lower selves are dangled before our minds and hearts, to seduce us into sin. Most of all to seduce us into the sin against the Holy Spirit, that tempts us to flee from the wilderness into a lifetime of busyness and bustle, that barricades the Holy One out altogether.

""Prayer is the place where repentance is learned through practicing repentance. It is in this process alone that the Holy Spirit can enter into your spirit, to re-fashion you into the man you have committed yourself to follow.

""Now go back to the mountain top where Jesus went to pray, and enter there through your prayer into His repentance, into His conflict with the power of evil that is within you. That is the only way to imitate Him, to welcome into your life the same Spirit who entered into His.'

""But surely Jesus didn't have to repent,' I said, 'that suggests that He was a sinner like us.'

""Oh no, it doesn't, my son. Only a sinner could draw such a conclusion,' said Brother Potentius with a smile. 'Sinners have only one understanding of repentance. For them it means to turn away from a sin that has been committed, and they usually associate it with feelings of guilt and remorse. Repentance means much more than that. Repentance means to turn away not only from sin, but from the temptations to sin; to turn away from the tempter who most certainly taunted the Savior Himself on this very mountain.'

'"As Easter drew near Brother Potentius and I set out for Jerusalem, leaving the ancient monastery by a narrow goat's track that led us down to a lonely rocky ravine at the foot of the mountain. We walked on in silence for many hours before he spoke again.

'"It would have been along this road that the Savior would have walked on His way to preach the repentance that He had already practiced Himself in the desert, and before,' said my master.

'"What do you mean by saying, "before?"' I asked. 'Did the Savior have to repent before He went into the desert?'

'"Oh you have indeed much to learn, my son — the Savior had been repenting for many years before He went into the desert.'

'"How so?' I said looking surprised and bewildered at the very idea.

'"Didn't the Savior have to grow, my son, didn't the muscles of His arms and legs have to grow and didn't His body have to grow too, so that he could learn to dress Himself, to feed Himself, to walk and talk, to work and to play.'

'"Yes, of course Master,' I replied.

'"Then didn't His mind and heart have to grow too?'

'"I suppose so — but I'd never thought of that before.'

'"Then you must go back to the Holy Book, and read there how He grew in wisdom and understanding with the years as He exercised the muscles of His mind — then read on, and you will see that he had come to do His Father's will, and that meant subjecting Himself to others, beginning with Mary and Joseph during the hidden years — and so He exercised the muscles of His heart, for many years before He went into the desert.

'"Repentance is but the word used by the Good Book to describe how love is learned, and received in its fullness.

'"Once Jesus had learned how to exercise His heart through years of selfless loving, then He could be filled with a love strong enough to sustain Him against all the wiles of the "wicked one."

""'Thank you Master.' I said. I never thought that the Savior had to learn loving as we do — but now I can see He chose to do everything that we have to do, to become our brother in every way.

""'Now my son you must learn that Satan did not leave the Savior when He left the desert, but he pursued Him, as He preached the repentance that He still had to practice Himself until He was glorified, and so as the Good Book says, He was tempted in every way as we are tempted.

""'Now notice that the Savior never preached that the Kingdom had come, only that it was near, that it was close at hand, that it was coming.

""'Only when He was glorified did the Kingdom of God's love fully sanctify the whole of His body, so that He could no longer even be tempted. When the first apostles preached they preached that the Kingdom had now fully come in the risen One, in His glorified body.

""'To enter this Kingdom, my son, you must imitate the Savior by doing what He did, by exercising your heart in prayer through repentance. That will allow the Spirit who raised Him on the first Easter Day to raise you also.'

""'We had taken the old road for Jerusalem that passes the legendary inn associated with the Good Samaritan. Indeed, we were just beyond this very place when we were joined by a fellow traveler also bound for the Holy City. Far from being a fellow pilgrim, he was an arrogant young man not much older than myself with an insolent air about him that was soon made even more manifest in his behavior.

""'Without any provocation he began making fun of Brother Potentius and myself, and poured ridicule upon the faith we obviously professed. Even when he made so bold as to attack the Savior Himself, Brother Potentius spoke not a word. I was left to my own meager devices in endeavoring to answer him.

""'What does Jesus Christ know about life?' he said, with a sneer. 'What does He know about the power of evil? Did He ever sin?'

""'No,' I replied emphatically. 'He did not.'

""Well, there you are then. He was a goody goody, and what's the use of a goody goody as a guide? How can He know what we have to go through? What does He know about the power of temptation that we have to experience — the power of evil that we come up against?'

"'I'm not suggesting that there was anything either supernatural or preternatural about what happened next, though here I differ from my master, but as we approached the Holy City there was an almighty clap of thunder, and a flash of lightning that cracked open the sky. The wind arose, as if from nowhere, directing the rain into our path with a force and fury that I have never since experienced. We were soaked to the skin, all three of us, by the time we huddled together for shelter in a tiny shepherd's hut on the side of the road..

"'It was then that we noticed a young shepherd making his way down the hill opposite us, and we gazed aghast at such persistence as he trudged forward, his body almost at right angles as he led his sheep up the road that we had wisely deserted.

"'For the first time Brother Potentius turned and gazed at our cocky companion as he watched the young shepherd.

"'Tell me,' he said, 'Who knows more about the power of the storm? You in here, or that young man out there?'

"'That fool out there, of course.'

"'Yes, you are so right,' said Brother Potentius. 'And that is why Jesus Christ knows more about the power of evil than you will ever know. What do you do when the storm of carnal desire presents itself to you?'

"'The smirk on the man's face was the only answer he gave.

"'Exactly, my friend, you give in. That is why you know nothing about the power of evil. Jesus was tempted in every way we are tempted. But He never gave in to those temptations. That is precisely why He knows more about the power of evil than anyone else who has ever walked upon the face of the earth.'

"'The young man was gone the moment the storm ended.

"'You see,' said Brother Potentius, 'sin is the safety valve used by sinners that prevents them experiencing the real power of evil. It is sin that prevents us from experiencing the full fury of hell that is within each of us. Try a little experiment for yourself, my son. Next time your brother pokes fun at you, say nothing. Accept all his ridicule in silence. No matter how he tantalizes you, refuse to use the safety valve of sin, and then I promise you you will experience the power of evil rising within you.

""It is the saint not the sinner who knows all about temptation and about the power of evil and sin. The sinner, who thinks he knows it all, knows nothing. It is in trying to resist temptation that you come to know its force, that you come to know just how irresistible that power is.

""No saint has yet been born into this world of ours who has not fallen, and fallen many times over, who has not used the safety valve of sin to save themselves from facing the fullest fury of the prince of darkness. But the Savior never used that safety valve, although He was tempted in every way as we are tempted. This is why He experienced more potently, more powerfully, than anyone to walk on the face of this earth, the full power and impact of the powers of darkness that were hurled against Him.

""Those first holy men to record the Savior's doings on earth saw Palestine as a battleground where the Prince of Peace had to confront the prince of this world. The power of evil gradually built up against the Savior with ever increasing fury, as the Holy Story reaches its climax. Notice it is the devil who enters into Judas. It is the Evil One who works through the princes of this world, through the high priests and the Sanhedrin, through Herod and his flatterers, through Pilate and the Roman soldiers. The terrible temptations that had taunted Him throughout His life on earth reach a terrible climax as He hangs naked and bleeding upon the Cross.

""Again and again He is tempted in pitch beyond pitch of grief; tempted to turn away from the path that has been laid out for Him by His Father. "If you are the Christ, come down from the Cross and we will believe in you." "He saved others but He cannot save Himself." And so He was tempted to the bitter end.

""In the last moments of His life upon earth He faced a storm more powerful than any, that ever was, or ever will be; a storm raised in the very bowels of hell by the monarch of mischief himself. One movement of Our Savior's fingers, and that storm would have been silenced. One glance of His eyes, and His tormentors would have been destroyed; one nod of that sacred head, and He would have come down from the Cross transfigured, with ten legions of angels at His side to defend Him.

""It is one thing, and a very great thing, to suffer for the truth when you have no choice, but to suffer in agony for the truth when you could end it instantly is a far greater thing still. That is true strength, not weakness, and to do that for others is true love, but to do that for those who would nevertheless betray you, is the height and depth, and the length and breadth, of a love that surpasses all understanding — and this is the love with which our Savior saved the world.

""In a short while, my son, we will be entering the Holy City where we will spend seven days till the day of the Lord's resurrection. Spend the time well, meditate upon all that you have seen and heard, for it is only in prayer that all the things we have spoken about will become clear to you.'

"'The strict discipline that I had had to endure in the desert was somewhat relaxed, as my master took me out every day during that Holy Week to explore the old city of Jerusalem with a jaunty good humor that made it a joy to be with him. I saw now why he was called Potentius 'the Pilgrim,' for his many sojourns in the sacred city had introduced him to every nook and cranny that had the slightest odor of sanctity about it. He strode the narrow highways and byways like an ancient patriarch, smiling benignly on tourist and tradesman alike, accepting many marks of respect bestowed upon him by a bewildering cross-section of Christians.

"'Some bowed low as he passed, others ran forward to kiss his hands, and several fell to the floor to kiss his feet. I felt proud to be his disciple.

"'On the Thursday of Holy Week he took me to the place

where the Savior celebrated the last supper with His disciples on the night before He died.

""'This is the place,' he said, 'where the Savior whom God had chosen to enter into human weakness, gathered human weakness around Himself in the men He had chosen to follow Him.'

""'But why does God always choose the weak?' I asked.

""'Because it has always been so from the beginning. Did He not choose a man of almost a hundred, and a barren woman of four score years and more to parent the promised people? Did He not choose the tongue-tied mutterer Moses to speak to the King of the Nile, the stripling David to fell the giant Goliath?

""'Why, oh why, my son?

""'To teach all that it is not this man's potency, nor that man's eloquence, nor was it a boy's strength, but the power of God at work through human weakness. This is the great mystery at the heart of our faith, this is why the Savior was born into weakness, as a helpless baby in a wooden crib, and this is why He died in weakness as a helpless man on a wooden cross — so that God's power could be seen as never before, raising Him into glory to be enthroned at the right hand of His Majesty to reign for ever in Light Inaccessible.

""'If you would follow Him, then you must learn to choose the weakness He chose for Himself and His followers. The Holy Peter who became the first of all His followers began as the least.'

""'The Savior called him Rock not because that's what he was but because that's what he was to become. It was a man made of jelly, not rock, who answered the call by the sea of Galilee. A man called Satan's son by the Savior Himself for having the temerity to tempt Him. A man who blustered and blundered his way into a final betrayal. But that was the man chosen, so that yet again all could see that God's Kingdom comes by none of man's working, but of God's working in man's weakness.

""'Learn from the Holy Peter, and mark well the way in which he repented. No matter how many times he fell, the moment he realized what he had done, no matter how low he had fallen, he had the humility to turn for forgiveness with a speed that thrust him forwards without delay towards the sanctity that he certainly did achieve.

""The key word is "speed." The difference between the saints and ourselves is not that they didn't fall and we do. It is that they had the humility to accept their weakness, and the moment they fell, they turned immediately for forgiveness without hesitation, without the delay before repentance that is always the measure of a person's pride. This was the apostle's saving grace, for in spite of the power of his preaching, the converts he made, and even the miracles he performed, he still fell many times over. For no event, however great, makes a saint save the event of a lifetime of repentance.

""Even though he fell out with the apostle Paul, refused to share the same table with Gentile converts, and still failed to see the true meaning of the Gospel, the very moment he realized his mistake he turned and opened himself to receive the Lord's forgiveness, so that gradually, by the power of the Holy Spirit, the man of jelly was solidified into the rock upon which God's Church was founded.'

""Master, you surprise me,' I said. 'For I thought that the twelve had all been sainted on the first Pentecost day, and now you tell me of two holy apostles at odds with each other.'

"'Brother Potentius laughed. 'You have still much to learn, my son. They were apostles, yes, but holiness is only won in a prolonged combat that they had not yet sustained. Don't think that a conversion on the Damascus road sainted the bigot whom God had chosen, as yet another fool with which to confound the wise. Conversion is a once or twice in a lifetime affair that sets a man on a new road, that is paved to Paradise with more moments of repentance than paces between Palestine and the Pontus.

""No saint is absolved from this journey, no matter how high the pedestal that they are finally set upon. See for yourself in the life of Paul; see his hot temper, his pride, his boastfulness. In the

Holy Book itself see him not once, but twice, in an unholy dispute with Barnabas and Mark, who were themselves sainted in the end. But like the apostle whose feast he shares, it was his humility that saved him. He was the first to write for others the great secret of the spiritual life that weakness is strength, for the fallen who rise repeatedly for the Savior's forgiveness. Though he falls seventy times, the Savior will raise him seventy times seven for he will not be found wanting in observing the commandment he enjoins upon others.

""It was Saint John who said that all men are sinners and the man who says he is not is deceiving himself, and calling the living God a liar. And this is so. But the apostle Paul was inspired to see that sin itself can become a stepping-stone to sanctity as it was in his own most holy search. Though the "sting of the flesh" sinned and shamed him throughout his life, it conditioned him to sanctity, for it was the continual reminder of his weakness, and so of his need for God, that led him to the "repentance without ceasing" that is the only sure way to sanctity.

""Remember this, my son, and mark it well, there is no word in the whole of Holy Writ for a man or a group of men who have repented, but only for those in the process of repenting. So repent without delay; repent without ceasing. This is the only way to sanctity. This is the only prayer that will always be heard and answered with the divinization which is the deepest desire of all true believers.

""When you stop falling, you will be in heaven, but when you stop getting up then you will be in hell.'

"'On the holiest of nights Brother Potentius arranged for me to spend the whole night in our monastery that is actually inside the Holy Sepulchre. When all the visitors had left, and the great doors had been bolted I went inside the tomb from which the Savior was raised to glory, and spent the night in prayer. There in that hallowed place I heard holy words that spoke to my heart with a clarity that remains with me to this day. I had been so overcome by the privilege that had been granted to me, that I prayed intensely that if it were the Savior's will I might remain there in that monastery for the rest of my life, so that I could return each night to pray at what is surely the most holy place on earth.

"'I had hardly finished my prayer when I heard these words quite clearly:

"''You are looking for Jesus of Nazareth who was crucified. He is risen. He is not here. See, here is the place where they laid Him. He has gone before you into Galilee. It is there that you will find Him.'

"'In a flash I knew that I would leave that place and never return again, nor would it matter, for now that the Lord had risen every place could be a holy place, if it is the place where the penitent is prepared to repent, to allow the Lord in.

"'I wanted to leave there and then, to begin my life anew, to learn repentance as the Savior had learned it, and then to preach that message to others.

"'I prayed again before I left that spot. This time it was a different prayer. 'Lord, reveal to me this day how best I can call others to the repentance that you preached, and that you have revealed to me so clearly.'

"'That prayer was answered that very day.

"'It was at the feet of our most venerable patriarch that I sat that Easter night with many other monks from far and wide, who had come to take part in the ceremonies over which he had presided and to listen to his words of wisdom that were in a special way spoken to me.

"'A group of monks, who had been discussing the Sacred Scriptures asked him to interpret a text from the prophet Ezekiel which they could not understand.

"''What is it that puzzles you, my brothers?' he asked them.

"''Well,' said one, 'the Man of God calls upon us all to preach repentance to everyone we meet, on whatever occasion we meet them, and then he warns us that if we do not do this, then one day we will be held to account for the sins that they fall into.'

"''And what is it that you do not understand, my brothers?

For it is the Holy Book that speaks, and it never speaks falsely.'

"'Our difficulty is this, venerable one,' said an elderly monk. 'The truth of the matter is that we don't preach repentance to all we meet, nor do we see how we can do so, and further, it doesn't seem fair that we should be called to account for the sins that they fall into.'

"'Listen, and listen carefully,' said the venerable patriarch. 'Know this. Only the Savior, the true Icon, the perfect image and likeness of God can call people to repentance. Repent yourselves, brothers, to admit God's Spirit within you. He alone will form you in the image and likeness of the Savior.

"'When all who meet you, see in you the Icon of the Savior Himself, they will want to change their lives in holy repentance, before ever you have opened your mouths. If you do not speak with the example of your life, brothers, it would be better if you did not speak at all, for to speak with the sound of your voice what is denied by the sight of your body is to be a hypocrite to whom no one will listen. Listen, all of you, and hear this — for the Risen One has no other image on earth than in those who choose to receive Him, and no voice with which to call others to Him than the voice that speaks to the world through you.'"

'Father Dimitrius smiled as he repeated the punch-line of his story, so that it would not be lost on me. He stood up and took me by the hand. "That will do for the present, my friend," he said. "I have always believed that the hand of God was upon me, and His holy voice spoke to me in a special way on that pilgrimage, and so whenever I feel it opportune to re-tell it to someone like yourself I do not attempt to embellish or to interpret it, for fear of disturbing holy ground.

"'Go away now and meditate upon all you have heard so that God can speak to you upon your way as He spoke to me upon my way. For though there is but one God, there are many ways to Him along the royal road of repentance."

'Father Dimitrius had answered for me far more questions than I had in fact asked. Not only had he shown me the inner meaning of the prayer, that I had thought meaningless, but he had introduced me into the meaning of repentance that had to be learned there, the repentance that would enable me to enter not just into the life of Christ but into His action so that the life that had progressively filled and then animated Him could likewise animate me. This was the way to true imitation.

'I returned to Paris from Paradise at the end of April to find that though the environs of this famous city may well be renowned the world over for the making of love between man and woman, it's not so conducive to the making of love between Man and God especially if your address happens to be Trois Place Pigalle, Montmartre.'

* * * * * * * * * *

I was still sitting, thinking over all that Peter had written in his typescript when Father James suddenly burst into the room.

"Are you ready to take off?" he said. "I've got all the provisions and they are already in the boat. Let's get moving. We'll be on Calvay by midday."

It was almost eleven **4** o'clock when we set
out for Calvay. Father James had attached a small spare boat to
his launch so that I could use it if needed to get back to the
mainland. He warned me only to use it if it was absolutely
necessary. Nevertheless, he showed me the safest channel to use
as we sailed along the narrow inlet that spanned half the distance
between Calvay and the presbytery.

As we emerged from the inlet Calvay was straight ahead of
us. It looked bare and forbidding in the dull, murky light of the
heavily overcast June morning. The tide was on its way out as we
both clambered out of the boat on to Peter's home-made jetty,
but the morning brightened as we walked along the path beside
the sea. The fluffy white highlanders, who were Peter's charges,
greeted our arrival with complete and almost insolent indifference.
Miraculously the sun burst through the clouds as we walked up
the slope towards Peter's cottage.

It's a strange country, the far North. At one moment it
exasperates you with prolonged periods of monotonous rain and
mist so that you may as well be blind for all the difference the
scenery makes. Days of unremitting and relentless rain make you
swear you'll never risk another holiday in that godforsaken place.
Then in a few unforgettable moments everything changes and
makes you renounce the vow you made the moment before. The
rain suddenly stops; the cloud lifts a little, and the late low-lying
sunset peers through the rising mist, to conjure colors of
indescribable tone and texture that simply take the breath away,

leaving you entranced for hours to come and staining your memory for a lifetime with a picture that can never fade.

This was one of those moments of magic. It almost seemed stage-managed with theatrical precision. The moment we mounted the ridge that straddled the island, the dull sulky landscape was instantly transformed and beamed back at the sun as it burst through the clouds. Two almost identical shorelines curved themselves round each side of the ridge, and arched round the headland, where they met to form a large sandy keyhole that shimmered and shone in the sunlight.

The beautiful symmetrical silver strand was surrounded on all sides by fluid ribbons of color in the sea that leaned and lapped into one another with ever changing purpose and intent. Almost every shade of blue and green could be seen, merging into one another with delightful effect. These predictable colors were broken up by lavish layers of maroon that unceremoniously burst into the monopoly, and struck a scene of such splendor, that no camera could ever capture, nor any artist reproduce without seeming to be facile or banal.

Several times before we reached the cottage the landscape changed without warning, from the somber to the sublime and back again, as the sun played hide-and-seek behind the clouds. It was as if some stage-designer was playing the fool with his sets, as he switched them to and fro with unpredictable timing from "Cinders in the Kitchen" to "Cinderella at the Ball."

I couldn't help but smile as we came close to the small thatched cottage that was Peter's home. There was something lovable and comic at the same time about it all. There was a funny little gate in front of it that looked as if it had had too much to drink, and was only prevented from the humiliation of total collapse by accepting the support of two old gate-posts. What I found most amusing was that both gate and gate-posts were quite superfluous, as there was no fencing of any sort, either round the house or anywhere else on the island for that matter.

"Well, there it is," said Father James, with a touch of pride as he stood still for a moment in front of Peter's island hermitage.

It was quite clear that Father James laid at least an emotional claim to the small Hebridean black-house that had once been the home of his ancestors.

When Father James had shown me the interior of the house and where everything was to be found, he left me to settle in and get down to work, promising to call in a day or two to see all was well.

The house was divided into two rooms. One served as a bedroom and a study, the other served as a kitchen and a sitting-room.

There was a big desk in the study with two large filing cabinets on either side, spanning the whole width of the room.

I unpacked as quickly as I could, made myself a cup of tea, and sat down to read Peter's next typescript. I simply couldn't wait to see how Peter had fared in Paris at the seedy sounding address of Trois Place Pigalle, Montmartre. It was entitled:

FROM MONTMARTRE TO MOSCOW

'There was a letter from my brother Tony awaiting me on my return to Paris. I thought it was to inform me of the date of his proposed marriage. Instead, it was to inform me of the date upon which he would enter the seminary. He had broken off his engagement, packed up his law studies at Manchester University, and been accepted for the priesthood by the Bishop of Salford.

'Tony was about a year older than I. We'd always been close and I'd always been able to talk to him about my own spiritual aspirations. He had admitted to me that he needed a close personal flesh-to-flesh love, as the background to the spiritual journey that was as important to him as it was to me. His sudden and unexplained change of direction was something of a shock, that made me stop to think of the direction my own life was taking. It seemed to have no purpose of late, save a rather haphazard searching that had led me to where I was by accident rather than by design. At least, that's how it seemed to me.

'I thought I must be a little more disciplined in my search to find my vocation in life. I decided that it would be impossible to make a proper decision without a deeper knowledge of the God to Whom I wished to commit myself. I couldn't be blamed if my religious education had been unsatisfactory in the past, but I could be blamed if I didn't do anything to rectify the situation in the future, and so I turned to the university chaplain for help.

'Anton, as he wanted to be called, was a charming and brilliant Dominican theologian with a string of degrees after his name. He had a tall athletic body that supported a bullet-shaped head with distinctive angular features that were framed by ginger sideburns, and a small pointed beard. Everyone liked him because he was one of the boys, always at the center of university life, whether it was debating the bomb in the university library, or discussing the merits of that year's vintage in the university bar. His pride and joy was a pre-war Simca that he had fitted with the latest souped-up sports engine, and he used to get endless delight out of leaving his fellow motorists standing, as the lights changed to green.

'I liked him, and we got on very well. I was mesmerized by his prodigious knowledge, and by the enthusiasm with which he set about my theological education.

'"Your basic ideas about the Renaissance are right," he said. "But as a total explanation of the current malaise in Christian spirituality, it is a little too simplistic. There are many other features that have to be taken into account that must be studied from a more systematic theological and historical perspective."

'Within a matter of days he had drawn up for me the study program that would take about three years to complete, and which was designed in such a way that it would not impinge on my secular studies.

'I will be eternally grateful to Anton for a theological education that distilled the best of the new and the old in a theological synthesis that he'd already made his own years before the Second Vatican Council.

'No other body of men made such a significant contribution to the Council than the French Dominican theologians. Many, like the great Yves Congar, had to pay the penalty so often reserved by the Church for being right too soon. It was a great privilege to meet many of these great men through Anton, to attend their lectures, read their works, and even take part in the great contribution that they made, by translating some of their works into English, and several into Russian.

'The great French Oratorian, Père Louis Bouyer, made perhaps the greatest impression on me. I attended all the lectures that he gave at the Institut Catholique and elsewhere, and read everything he wrote.

'In the Easter of my second year, my youngest brother, David, came to Paris for a month as part of a cultural exchange program. Bernard, his French pen-pal, had already stayed at our home in Manchester the previous summer. David brought hot news with him, for Tony had left the seminary, and had already been accepted by the Provincial of the Franciscan Order. It seems he'd read a book about Saint Francis that had set him thinking. Still more reading, coupled with advice from his spiritual director, convinced him that this is what God wanted him to do.

'I must say I didn't know much about Saint Francis, except that he preached to birds, tamed wolves and preached about Lady Poverty, whoever she was. His confrere, Saint Anthony, meant much more to me. I think I would have ended up in the debtor's prison without his uncanny way of finding things that I had usually given up for lost before turning to him as a last resort.

'The older I got the less I liked praying to saints to do things for me, but I couldn't get over the fact that without him I'd have lost for good my watch, one wallet with a hundred pounds in it, and my check book, and that was only in the last three months! If God was calling me to embrace Lady Poverty, it was quite obvious Saint Anthony hadn't heard about it!

'Towards the end of my third year Anton invited me to go with him to a lecture on prayer given by the great Benedictine preacher Archbishop Arnou to the priests of the diocese of Paris. I'm glad I was able to write down almost everything he said, because he had the ability to convey such profound theological truths in such a simple way that even I could understand. Instead of re-telling what he said in my words, let me rather reproduce my notes exactly as they were written, so that his words can speak for themselves.

ARCHBISHOP ARNOU ON PRAYER

'Some years ago I was called to Rome to take part in a seminar on prayer for Benedictines from all over the world. I found myself in the unenviable position of having to act as chair-person to a group of twenty or so abbots and abbesses. I was wondering how to get the ball rolling when I suddenly hit on the idea of asking each person to put in their own words what they considered to be the essence of prayer. One said it was having a conversation with God, another that it was about being open to Him; another suggested it had more to do with listening than anything else, while others resorted to the old "penny catechism" — prayer is the raising of the heart and the mind to God.

'When everybody had had their say, an abbess from the United States suddenly stood up at the back and demanded that I should make a contribution before going any further. Well, being a diplomat, I gave a very diplomatic answer. I said I agreed with everybody, because everybody had been saying more or less the same thing, but that I would like to add one word to qualify every phrase, every sentence that had been used. It was the simple word "trying." Prayer is *trying* to have a conversation with God, *trying* to be open to God, *trying* to listen to Him, *trying* to raise the heart and mind heavenward. It's all in the trying. This is the very essence of prayer.

'Imagine two people going to pray. The first person spends their time sitting there like a "suet pudding" waiting to be soaked in syrup. The second is swept up in an ecstasy for half an hour, totally absorbed in God; neither are really praying. In the first case, the person does absolutely nothing, and in the second case God does absolutely everything. Prayer is in between the suet pudding and the ecstasy. It's the place where the trying is done, by a person who keeps endeavoring to turn their heart's gaze towards God despite the distractions that endeavor to turn them elsewhere.

'When I turned to God in prayer this morning, I wanted to remain absorbed in Him alone, to be enveloped in the peace that surpasses all understanding, but two seconds after starting I was lost in distractions. As soon as I realized what was happening, I turned my attention back to God, but once again, a few seconds later I was lost once more in distractions.

'I started debating in my mind whether to spend the summer holidays with my niece and her family at their villa in Monte Carlo or with my aunt at her semi in Liverpool! Once again I tried to turn back to God, only to find yet again that my attention was drawn elsewhere — should I accept the invitation to give a retreat in California, or go to the Synod in Rome? I know what I'd like to do, but this might be my last chance to charm my way into a red hat!

'If your experience in prayer is anything like mine, then take heart, I've got good news for you. Saint Teresa of Avila said that we will always have distractions in prayer, at least this side of the grave. It is a great mistake to believe that distractions are a sign that you can't pray, for what does it mean if you have a hundred and one distractions in say half an hour of prayer? It means that one hundred and one times you've turned away from distractions and turned back to God. It means that you have repented one hundred and one times. It means that you have repeatedly said "No" to self and "Yes" to God, performed a hundred and one acts of selfless loving that have enabled you to die to the "Old Man" so that the "New Man" can be formed.

'This is why a great mediaeval mystic called prayer the *Schola Divini Amoris* or the School of Divine Love, because it is the place where a person freely chooses to go, in order to learn the most important lesson that a human being can ever learn, and that is, how to love, and it is learned by practicing selfless loving, in set periods of time put aside for that purpose.

'There is no mystery about the learning process. It is based on the old principle "practice makes perfect."

'If you want to learn how to cook, learn a foreign language or even how to drive a car, it takes time and it takes practice. Prayer is the place where we set aside concentrated periods of time to learn how to become selfless lovers. Like all other forms of learning, it involves performing series after series of selfless actions before ever a habit is learned. It leads us on to gain the inner facility of selflessness, that is the only authentic sign of sanctity.

'No one will ever learn anything without putting time aside for continual practice, in concentrated periods of time set aside for that purpose. Learning to love in the *Schola Divini Amoris* is no exception to the rule.

'So far I have been stressing the word "trying," but in Christian spirituality the *way* in which a person tries is more important still. If *trying* is the heart of prayer, then *gentleness* is the soul of prayer. The gentle way in which you start again, no matter how many times you fail in prayer, breathes the breath of humility into the very way in which you try. It is the humility of one who knows their weakness, knows that they will fail time and time again, but is never deterred from starting anew no matter how many times they may fall.

'It is the arrogant who are angered by failure, who knit their brows, grit their teeth and clench their fists in an endeavor to batter down the gates of heaven. They are angry, not because they have failed God, but because they have failed themselves, and the great ideals that they have set for themselves. Whenever you find yourself getting angry with your failure in prayer, be sure that it is your own pride that has been injured. The humble person is never surprised by failure, nor do they delay in beginning again to turn back to the only One Who can bring strength out of weakness.

'What is true of prayer is true of the whole of the spiritual journey. We are all sinners, and we will fall until the day we die. Success does not consist in not falling, so much as in continually getting up. It's all in the getting up, or more precisely in the gentle way in which we get off the ground to start again, sorry for having fallen but never surprised.

'I have not chosen to use the word "trying" and the word "gently" on a passing whim, but because these two words, harnessed together, help to balance two major theological trends that have dominated Christian spirituality. The older Orders associated themselves with the Dominican school of thought that pre-dated the rise of humanism in Europe, and so quite naturally they lay particular emphasis on the action of God, while the Orders founded after the rise of humanism, tended to associate themselves with the Jesuit school, that predictably emphasized the action of Man. Naturally, both are orthodox, but both have inbuilt dangers that we must be aware of. The Dominican school can so emphasize the action of God, and what He can do, that they can forget what they should be doing, and so fall into a sort of practical quietism. In its turn this can lead to a presumption that dissipates the heart and mind, and finally the whole person. On the other hand the Jesuit school can place such faith in Man, and what he can do, that they forget what God does, at least in practice, and so they are led into a sort of practical semi-pelagianism. In its turn this leads to pride; to an arrogance of heart and mind that destroys everything they try to do.

'I have introduced you to the word "trying" to minimize the danger of falling into the presumption of practical quietism, and to the word "gently" to minimize the danger of falling into the pride of semi-pelagianism.

'Harness these two words together, and they should lead you into what you will forgive me calling Benedictine moderation.

'Prayer life, like the spiritual life, is all a question of balance, the balance between two extremes. It's like walking a tight-rope with pride on one side and presumption on the other, and the best of us spend a lifetime falling off, at one moment into semi-pelagianism, and at another into quietism. We read a book that excites us, attend an exhilarating retreat, or meet an inspiring person, and we are suddenly spurred into action. We get out the "hair shirts," start fasting, keeping vigils and praying half the night — then, when we end up exhausted, we turn into spiritual layabouts again, waiting on God with a cigarette in one hand, a drink in the other, and our feet up in front of the telly!

'True balance is ultimately the gift of the Holy Spirit, a gift that is given to a person in the process of "gently trying" to pray. Now it is possible to see a little more accurately the essence and the inner meaning of prayer. Prayer is a process of continual inner conversion that involves gently trying to turn, open and surrender the heart to God. As the process is practiced, the heart of man is made accessible to the heart of God, and His love shafts down to purify and empty it, so that Christ can come to birth again in all of us.

'I don't want to start hair-splitting but I think it is very important to distinguish between what is the essence of prayer and what are means to prayer. People are always asking me to advise them what method of prayer to adopt, or more usually to bless the prayer pattern that they have already adopted. Some people fritter away their lives searching for the spiritual equivalent of the Philosopher's Stone, the magic formula for prayer, that will infallibly lead to mystical contemplation, or to whatever other spiritual "goodies" they have set their hearts on.

'The truth of the matter is there is no perfect means of prayer. There are just different means, to help a person to keep gently trying, to turn and open their heart to the only One Who can make them new. Methods and techniques of prayer are like props. Their purpose is to help a person to keep on loving, to keep turning back to God. If the Rosary helps to do this, if the Stations of the Cross, or some other devotional practice helps to do this, then that's fine. Others may find the slow meditative reading of the Scriptures helpful, or using a word or a phrase as suggested by the author of *The Cloud of Unknowing*.

'Generations of believers have found the Jesus prayer most suitable for them. The important point to remember is there is no magic formula, no infallible methods or techniques. There are just hundreds of different ways of prayer to do one and the same thing. A means of prayer is good for you if it helps you, here and now, to keep gently turning your heart back to God. What might help you at the beginning of your spiritual journey may be of no use later on. What helps you in the morning might not help you in the evening. What helps you one minute might not help you the next. So please move from one method to another with complete freedom. Remember that these methods are only means. Beware of the here today and gone tomorrow Gurus, who have a fetish about a particular means of prayer, which they enjoin upon everybody without question as a "panacea."

'They know nothing about the spiritual life. If they did they'd know that methods of prayer change as people change and as prayer develops with the years. A good spiritual director like a good doctor has to make some form of diagnosis before they can determine what course of action to recommend.

'What would you think if your doctor handed out pink pills to every patient without bothering to examine them? You'd think he was a "quack" and you would be right. Medical quacks used to be commonplace in the past, but spiritual quacks are far more commonplace today.

'I would like to end this talk by putting the microscope upon the greatest mystic who has ever walked upon the face of this earth, to catch Him in the act of praying, so that we can see yet again, this time even more clearly, the essential ingredients of authentic Christian prayer.

'At the end of His life Jesus knew that His hour had come. He knew that in a short time He was going to be betrayed by one of His own. He was going to be dragged in front of the Jewish authorities to be accused of being a blaspheming liar. He was going to be dressed like a fool and paraded in front of that debauched dilettante Herod. He was going to be stripped by the Romans, flogged literally within an inch of His life, dragged through the streets like a common criminal, and then hung up, naked and bleeding, to die on a Roman gibbet. His humanity rebelled at the very thought of it; He was in desperate need and so now, in His hour of greatest need, he turned for help to His Father in prayer.

'He goes into the garden "where it was His custom to pray," and there throws Himself down upon the ground to beg for the help and strength to remain steadfast to the end. Then He tries to turn and open Himself to receive that help and strength from the Father, but He is overwhelmed by a thousand and one distractions, taunted by temptations that threaten to come between Him and the love of His Father whom He needs so desperately at this, His moment of greatest need.

'Where do the temptations come from? What is the source from which these temptations arise? They come from the same place as our distractions. They rise from the same source as our temptations. They come from the memory, from the imagination, from the inner sensual feelings that all batten upon the mind, bludgeoning it with blows that all but batter it into submission.

'First of all His memory looks back over almost thirty years. How many times in those years had He come to Jerusalem? How many times had He approached other major cities in Palestine, and seen there on the garbage heap outside the city gates slaves, criminals, malefactors of every sort hung up on post and cross-beam, half flayed alive, slowly choking to death. Then His imagination comes into play as He begins to imagine that this will be happening to Him the next day. He begins to realize more poignantly than ever the atrocious agony that He will have to endure at the hands of His own people, and before the loving gaze of those who love Him most. He is bathed in blood, sweat and tears, and His deepest feelings are aroused and they rise up to batter His mind, beleaguer it with a thousand and one questions. Why? For what purpose? Or at least, why this way, and not another?

'The temptation to take a short cut that had already tested Him in the desert, tests Him now to the limits of His endurance so that He begins to pray, "Father, if it be possible, let this chalice pass away from Me." Then the Holy Spirit enables Him to pray time and time again, "Yet not My will but Your will be done," until He becomes the prayer He makes, the will of God made flesh.

'This is real prayer. This is the highest form of prayer in which the inner repentance of Jesus was brought to perfection as He relentlessly turned and opened Himself to the Father, and was repeatedly emptied of every thought, word and desire that stood in the way of the total surrender that He made and re-made in that hallowed place.

'The angel of consolation who came to comfort and support Him brought moments of light to His darkness, to give Him the help and strength to go on surrendering Himself in prayer, so that in the process of His final prayer of repentance He was given the power and the strength to go out of that garden, to bring the repentance He had preached to others to perfection in the final moments of His life on earth. This time He would repent, not just with His heart, but with His bloodied hands and His feet, with His lacerated head, His tortured body and the whole of His personality. What was learned with the heart in Gethsemane was put into practice with His whole being on Calvary.

'Now we can see the real meaning and inner nature of Christian prayer; see how it is the school in which the heart is trained, disciplined in the selflessness that leads us into the selfless sacrificial prayer of Jesus. It is the place where we learn to participate in His death and resurrection. It is the place where true imitation leads to an identification that enables the Risen One to be present to the world through us.

* * * * * * * * * *

'I was so impressed by the singer, as well as the song, that I started to think seriously about a vocation in the monastic life, and spent several weekends at Citeaux, where I was to try my vocation at Mount Saint Bernard's, the Cistercian monastery in England.

'However, events took a different turn as I will shortly relate. It was while I was at Citeaux one weekend that I met a very holy priest, who, as it turned out, lived only a mile from me in Paris. He so impressed me that I began to go to him for confession and spiritual direction for the remainder of my student days. His name was Père Jacques Le Bec.

'He was a Carmelite, who had spent most of his life a slave to the confessional. Four years in the trenches during the First World War had left him a cripple for life, with an infected foot that had to be dressed each day, and which confined him to a wheelchair.

'For Père Le Bec it had been a school for sanctity. A sanctity that attracted people of every sort to seek him out as a confidante and spiritual director. From the side he looked exactly like General de Gaulle on wheels, but the moment he turned to greet you the impression immediately vanished. Suddenly he became everyone's favorite uncle, warm, welcoming, full of fun and good humor.

'There was at first no hint of the holiness that held together the most balanced personality I have ever met. We took to each other immediately. Perhaps it was my own physical disability that drew us together into a relationship of personal friendship that enhanced the spiritual direction he was able to give me, by enabling me to be completely open with him from the start.

'I went to see Père Le Bec once a fortnight, and he guided my prayer life with consummate care and skill. It was through him that I was gradually introduced to the writings of the great Carmelite mystics, Saint John of the Cross and Saint Teresa of Avila, though he was insistent that I should read only what he recommended and no more.

'There was no change in the general pattern of my prayer. It was still as dark as ever even at the best of times, and I always had to battle against thousands of distractions that prevented me from attaining the inner peace of heart and mind that I desired with all of my being. But you can bear almost anything if it has a meaning, and Père Le Bec showed me quite clearly the meaning and purpose of traveling on bravely in "the dark night of the soul." Then a new and startling development took place that was to have a lasting impression on my spiritual journey.

'It had been my custom to go to the chapel in the university or to a favorite corner in Notre Dame. It was in the early June of my last year with my friend Boris in Paris that something happened when I was at prayer in the famous cathedral that had a determining influence on the rest of my life.

'Although I got nothing out of my daily prayer, I nevertheless persevered as Père Le Bec had taught me, using the Jesus prayer as best I could to ward off the distractions and temptations, that were my most faithful companions, as I tried to fix my gaze upon God as best I could — then things suddenly changed dramatically in the space of a few days.

'For two nights on the run I found myself wrapped in a deep inner recollection that was quite clearly not self-imposed. Then on the third day I experienced a lifting inside my head that raised me up above myself, or rather raised my consciousness to a high degree of awareness. I knew without a shadow of a doubt that I had nothing to do with this new development in my prayer life. For the next three nights the same experience enveloped me.

'On the fourth night the lifting sensation that I had experienced before was intensified tenfold. This time I soared, spiraling upwards in my mind, to such a high degree of consciousness that I knew I would have experienced complete oblivion if the intensity had increased by a single degree. I was so totally absorbed in God that I had no distractions at all. This was the pattern of my prayer life for the next week or more, as the awareness of God's action within me rose and fell with varying degrees of intensity, that had nothing whatsoever to do with me and my puny efforts.

'The effect of these experiences on my spiritual life was as dramatic as the experiences themselves. I felt humbled, not proud, by the power of God, totally unworthy and yet utterly grateful at the same time. I wanted to commit myself to God and to His will more perfectly than ever before, even if it literally meant Gethsemane for the rest of my life and the Cross at the end of it.

'I knew then that as long as the power of God worked in my weakness I would be able to do anything, just as without it I would be able to do nothing. I could only marvel at the insight and wisdom of Père Le Bec as I looked back upon the way he reacted to the new development in my prayer life. He showed no signs of surprise at all; took it all as quite normal and to be expected. He could have taken the opportunity to introduce me to Saint Teresa's *Interior Castle*, but he was far too wise for that. Instead he pulled out a copy of the *Confessions* of Saint Augustine and read out the following passage:

'"When first I knew you, you lifted me up so that I might see that there was something to see, but that I was not yet the man to see it, and you beat back the weakness of my gaze, blazing upon me too strongly and I was shaken with love and with dread, and I knew that I was far from you in the region of unlikeness, as if I heard your voice from on high. I am the food of grown men; grow and you shall eat me."

'Père Le Bec took both of my hands in his and gazed at me with eyes laden with love and compassion, and said, "Peter, you have been given these graces not because you are strong, but because you are weak, to strengthen you, to journey on the way that will lead you further into the desert where an ever deepening purification will prepare you for a more permanent intimacy with God. What you have experienced in your mind will be extended to every part of your personality, as Christ is being fully formed within you."

'Although the experiences continued for a few more weeks, they stopped almost as suddenly as they started. I blamed myself at the time and no doubt I was partially to blame, but I had no choice. The academic year was coming to its end; Boris was preparing to go back to Russia and I was busily employed looking for new digs for the following year to make use of the grant I had received for a year's research.

'I couldn't attend my brother's first profession as I would have liked because I had promised to spend the summer in Moscow with Boris, helping him to find and move into a new home with his ageing father, whom he had vowed to look after until he died before following his own monastic vocation on Mount Athos.

"It took all summer to get Boris and his father settled into their new home in Moscow. I was delighted to have the opportunity to meet so many committed Christians through Boris, whose deep faith put my own to shame. It was as if I'd been transported back in time to the early days of the Church when the blood of the martyrs had been the seed of the Church. Despite great suffering and the possibility of imminent transportation to labor camps, if not worse, Christians from every walk of life practiced their faith with a fortitude that left me in no doubt that the Church was more alive in Russia than anywhere else I had ever been. When I returned to Paris it was to my old lodging in Place Pigalle, for I had been unable to find anywhere else as suitable, or rather as cheap, in the time available.

'The first thing I did on my return was to write to my brother Tony to apologize for not being able to visit him since he had joined the Franciscan Order, but assuring him that I would come for Christmas to his new home, the student house at East Bergholt in Suffolk. It was a home, too, and he was completely at home there, and, as I was soon to discover, so was I, in the place where I found at last just what I had been looking for for years.'

* * * * * * * * * *

I spent an hour or so flipping through the content of Peter's filing cabinets to get some idea of the workload that lay ahead, and then I suddenly began to feel hungry; it was almost mid-afternoon and I'd eaten nothing since breakfast.

Father James's house-**5** keeper had made a packed lunch so I took it with me to eat outside. I settled down on a flat rock, about halfway between the cottage and the shore, and I began to reflect over the three typescripts I had just read but, as so often happens, I was sidetracked by my own uncontrollable imagination.

I began to day-dream. In no time at all I was lost in a Walter Mitty world of my own making. I was imagining myself as a spiritual Columbus of the twentieth century, discovering a new world of almost limitless spiritual riches and making them available to everyone. Maybe I could publish all his writings and shine with Peter's reflected glory.

A simply gorgeous bouncy little rabbit suddenly attracted my attention, and saved me from slipping any further into the childish fantasy world that was threatening to engulf me. He was skipping and scampering around his mother on the foreshore in front of me. The cheeky little imp would suddenly dash up to Mum, and snuggle in close for a free feed, before rushing away again to gambol playfully in the grass that skirted the sandy bay.

I couldn't help smiling at the earnest way he began to burrow into a patch of sand with all four paws. When he paused for a moment's respite, the whole area around his little snout was covered with sand. He glanced back at his mother, looking for all the world like a naughty three-year-old who had been caught in the act of raiding the chocolate biscuits, but his mother's attention was engaged elsewhere. Her soft, motherly bearing had suddenly stiffened; she was tense and nervous. I thought that she had become aware of my movements as I ate my lunch no more than thirty yards away, but no. Then I began to sense something. I couldn't put my finger on it at first. It wasn't so much the sense of fear that seemed to grip the rabbit, it was more a sense of impending presence that took hold of me.

I looked around but I couldn't see anything, or anyone to explain the atmosphere that seemed to over-shadow us. At last the little rabbit got the message from Mum; the mischievous sparkle faded from his eyes and in an instant both had vanished into the safety of their underground home.

Once more I looked round. The sheep continued to graze as before, but there was a difference. Though their heads were bowed low, and though they continued eating, they no longer relished what they ate, their minds were elsewhere. It was their eyes that were the giveaway; they glanced nervously upwards, though their mouths continued to chew as before.

I turned round, following their gaze into the sky, and there to my amazement and delight I saw a huge golden eagle no more than a hundred yards away and as many feet from the ground. Its head and shoulders were set hard into the strong prevailing wind that blew in over the headland. Its vast, shaggy wings spread imperiously out to leave you in no doubt that here in person was the Lord of the Isles. He remained almost motionless, staring impassively out to sea. Although he gave no sign, he was well aware of the effect his presence was having on the humbler inhabitants of the Island.

All the other birds seemed to have vanished; they had cautiously retreated to every nook and cranny from where they could safely regard their powerful overlord with fearful reverence and awe. I had never seen such a superb specimen before though in past years I had trekked for miles over barren mountains and boggy moorlands in the hope of a distant glimpse of this magnificent bird.

There was a hush, a sense of quiet that enveloped the whole

island. The very blades of grass seemed to waver against their will, and even the little cottage appeared to lower itself upon its haunches, not daring to move or flex the merest muscle that might attract the attention of the mighty bird of prey. Then all eyes stared incredulously. Even the breeze held its breath as a tattered old crow, the Island idiot, fluttered and flapped its way upwards and above the great bird. In a grotesque attempt at a dive, the clumsy creature had the audacity to try and mob the eagle single-handed. Just one stroke of those terrible talons would have been enough to send the simpleton to the ground senseless, but the great Lord of the Isles wasn't going to demean himself by doing to death a mindless minion before a motley group of peasants. The slightest movement of his great wings was enough to send the imbecile sprawling downwards in humiliating disarray.

Twice more the pathetic creature attempted to repeat his dangerous ploy with the same embarrassing result each time; but enough was enough. Without warning the mighty eagle began to rise higher and higher over the headland with hardly perceptible motion to more than a thousand feet, far beyond the idiot's reach. Then, before I could get back to the cottage for my binoculars, he had disappeared over Eriskay, heading towards the rugged easterly coast land of Uist.

I was simply thrilled. I had never imagined, even in my wildest flights of imagination, that I would ever see my favorite bird of prey at such close quarters, nor have the good fortune to witness the scene that had just been enacted before me. I stood gazing to the north for a long time after the speck had disappeared from my view. Then I turned to make my way back to the cottage. I had had a busy few days and I felt tired.

After a rather long siesta, I made myself an evening meal and then settled down to read Peter's next typescript. It was entitled:

FROM EAST BERGHOLT TO EAST DIDSBURY

'I only saw my brother for a few brief moments before

Christmas because, together with the other students, he was engaged in a whirlwind of activity, preparing for the great feast that had, as I was later to learn, a special place in Franciscan spirituality.

'There were practices, not just for the plain chant and polyphony but for the play and the pantomime, all of which I was destined to savor with various degrees of seriousness as the Christmas celebrations got under way. I had come across the phrase "Franciscan charity" in a purely secular literature, but I had never experienced it myself until that Christmas.

'I was immediately accepted as one of the family by everyone. I felt as if I'd known all the friars for years, and they accepted me as a brother without any of the phony affectation that so often characterizes religious communities, who are so busy trying to put on Christ that they usually put you off Him for years.

'The Christmas celebrations were so hectic, but so enjoyable, that it was a week before Tony and I could sit down for a serious talk, yet without that week in which I'd experienced for myself the brotherhood which he was to talk about with such enthusiasm, I don't think I would have been able to appreciate precisely what had attracted him to join the Franciscans. Tony had all the looks in our family and the brains too. There was a film-star quality about his appearance that turned heads wherever he went, and hearts too for that matter, but I never felt jealous or envious, I was far too busy being proud that he was my brother.

'"What on earth brought you here?" I said to him, as we sat down in his room that commanded a beautiful panoramic view of the Suffolk countryside.

'"Nothing on earth," Tony answered, grinning. "I suppose you thought I would have been married with a couple of kids by this time. Well, I suppose I would have been but for the pull that kept drawing me away from the marriage that everybody had been expecting. The strange thing was that it wasn't that I didn't love Beryl, it was just that something, or perhaps I should say Someone else, seemed to be drawing me elsewhere, and this Someone else kept getting between us. Eventually I had to break off the engagement, pack up my studies at the university and go to Ushaw College, Durham, to study for the priesthood.

"'However, even that wasn't enough because the pull that made me want to give myself to God in a more radical way was still there, but I didn't know what to do or how to go about it until I read Chesterton's *Saint Francis of Assisi.* It moved me deeply, moved me to search out the saint's own writings and read them for myself. I read them at a single sitting but they didn't impress me much. They just seemed to be a collection of letters and semi-canonical documents with a handful of admonitions, and a poem or two, that didn't do much for me at all.

"'The Franciscan sources were more interesting because they were full of stories, but they didn't seem to hang together into anything that touched me with the sort of inspiration that I suppose I was looking for. I felt like a heap of dry faggots, looking for a spark to set me aflame, but I couldn't seem to find it.

"'It was then that my spiritual director told me that I would never understand any spirituality properly unless I saw it in the context of the history into which it was born. So once again I went back to my books. I came to see that Francis had been responsible for an incredible and unique 'back to the Gospel' spirituality, that put Christ back at the center of Christianity and popular devotion, enshrining Him once more in the hearts and minds of ordinary people."

"'What you say interests me,' I said, "but I don't quite follow what you mean by saying Christ was put back at the center of Christianity. How could He have been anywhere else?"

"'Well, that's what I thought to begin with, but with the help and the guidance of my spiritual director I came to see that a very early heresy had completely distorted authentic Christian spirituality. You see, in the early days of the Church the first Christians were dominated by the great event of the Resurrection, not just because it was a world-shaking miracle, but because it was a sign that Jesus was no longer dead but alive. His new form of life raised Him up above the world of space and time to which we belong, and at the same time enabled Him to be inside it, in a new way, through love, so that He could be at the heart and center of all and every Christian community at one and the same time.

"'For the early Christians Christ was their Brother, and it was His brotherly love, or the Holy Spirit, which bound them all together into a brotherhood that Jesus Himself had prayed for at the Last Supper. It was the quality of the love that bound those early Christians together, that enabled them to show by the example of their own lives, that the Brotherhood of Man was not just a pipe-dream, but a real possibility for all who would accept Jesus as their brother by allowing His brotherly love to bond them together as a family. The trouble began when a man called Arius said Jesus was not God, but only a man.

"'The heresy eventually spread so far and wide that the majority of Christians became tainted with this travesty of the truth. In order to proclaim orthodoxy and stamp out Arianism the Church coined the slogan 'Christ is God,' and repeated it with such vigor, that when victory finally came Christ and God were hardly distinguishable in people's minds.

"'Christ, our Brother, who had been at the heart and center of Christian spirituality, had psychologically ascended into heaven in ordinary people's minds, and even some of the most important Christian writers used the word Christ for God, and God for Christ, without finding it necessary or important to distinguish one from the other.

"'Once the warmth, the closeness, and the humanity of Brother Jesus stopped drawing Christians out of themselves, then they started to look within, and rather unhealthy introspection made believers over-conscious of themselves and of their personal sinfulness.

"'As they seemed to be deprived of the spiritual resources they needed to reach up to God then they began to turn to their own human resources instead.

"'Under the influence of Greek ideas that flourished a

thousand years before the Renaissance, Christians began to adopt questionable ascetical practices, to free their souls from their sinful bodies that prevented them from raising themselves to God, or at least so they thought.

"'The repeated failures that always dog the do-it-your-self behavior generated a spiritual insecurity that led Christians to turn to others more worthy than themselves to represent them before God. The new devotions to the martyrs, the confessors, the saints, and our Lady, that grew with the passing years, became a measure of the distance that Christians felt separated them from the Jesus who had once been so close.

"'Another heresy, Macedonianism, did for the Holy Spirit what Arianism had done for Jesus, and so the brotherly love of Brother Jesus, the bond that united the first Christian communities together, seemed to disappear from Christian spirituality, if not in theory then certainly in practice, and that's what really matters. With God and Christ far away in heaven, and the Holy Spirit out of sight it's no wonder Christian community life suffered.

"'Rip out the cog from the wheel of a bicycle and see the effect it has on the spokes, and you'll see how without Christ at its center Christian community life was disastrously damaged, and it resulted in an unholy individualism that was quite uncharacteristic of the Church Christ originally founded.

"'Long before Francis was born, the Church that had once seemed like a warm all-embracing circle of love, with Christ at its center, began to look more like an austere pyramid with the God-Man at its summit and sinful man at its base. The sheer slopes only seemed scalable by intensive human endeavor, albeit with gifts of grace from the top, or with the help of other more saintly souls, who'd already reached the heights.

"'Obviously, I'm making sweeping generalizations, so that you can see at a glance something of the scene that Francis was going to reshape.

"'In one inspired step he was able to stride back over a thousand years to rediscover for himself the Gospel in all its simplicity, then share it with his brothers in the community that he founded, and with the world he had committed himself to serve."

"'All this is totally new to me,' I admitted. 'I've never heard it before.'

"'It was all new to me, too,' said Tony. "You see, Francis brought Christ back into the heart of Christian spirituality in such a decisive and effective way, that everybody has taken it for granted that that's how it has always been from the beginning, but it hasn't."

"'I had no idea that Francis was such a brilliant man,' I said.

"'No, he wasn't a brilliant man,' said Tony, "if by brilliant you mean a man of great intellectual ability or learning. He was a very simple man, a man of his time, but a man who was so totally open to God that he was able to see something with great simplicity that was denied to the great intellectual geniuses of his time. Because he was a man of his time, he was caught up and inspired by a great movement that completely dominated the spiritual sensibilities of his fellow Christians.

"'You see less than a hundred years before he was born, the whole of Europe had been inspired by a noble Christian ideal to go and win back the holy places from the infidels, who had held them for centuries. Encouraged by the Church, people from every walk of life set out for the East in pursuit of this holy ideal. Sovereigns and serfs, troops and troubadours, pious prelates and prostitutes, indeed the whole of Europe was brought to a fever pitch of excitement that is difficult to imagine a thousand years later.

"'A great man like Saint Bernard was preaching the Crusade only a few decades before Francis was born. He inspired men to give their lives for this noble cause by telling tales already coming back to the West of the places associated with the Savior's life, here on earth. By the time Francis was growing up, the family firesides, the taverns, the market-places as well as the courts of the nobility were places where tales were told and re-told of the places sanctified by the Savior.

"'The traveling troubadours had come back from the East with new instruments as well as new songs to sing, not only of courtly love and the deeds of the noble knights, but of the heavenly love of God, and of the places where that love had touched the world of Man.

"'No wonder it was one of Francis's deepest desires to go to the Holy Land himself. Nor was it surprising that when he came back he wanted to burn into the hearts of all men something of the fire that had set him alight with the love of the Lord of all, who chose to come in our midst as a helpless baby on that first Christmas Day.

"'This is why he built for himself and his fellow countrymen a crib in the hills of Greccio, high up above the Rieti Valley, and invited all who could to join him in a celebration of the Savior's birth that stained their memories with an experience that would inspire their hearts for a lifetime.

"'The cribs that found their way into every Christian home from that time onwards symbolized the re-birth of Christ's humanity into the heart of Christian spirituality, through the inspirational genius of the poor man of Assisi. But this wasn't the end of the great vision of Francis. It was in one sense only the beginning of a unique and all-embracing vision that was more profound than any before or since.

"'You see, he was dumbfounded by the world-shaking fact that the masterpiece of God's own creation, the King for Whom and in Whom the whole world was created, had freely chosen to become that helpless child, so that He could become a Brother to all men, Friar Jesus as he called Him. If all the world was created in Friar Jesus, then naturally all the world must be a friary. The Greek philosopher Plato had said, all the world is a prison, and the men and women in it no more than prisoners. The English dramatist Shakespeare said all the world's a stage, and the men and women merely players, each playing their part. The President of the United States said, all the world is a market-place, and the men and women merely buyers and sellers. But for Francis of Assisi all the world was a friary, and everyone and everything within it were naturally brothers and sisters to one another.

"'It's not just Brother Francis and Sister Clare, then, but Brother Sun and Sister Moon, Brother Wolf and Sister Lamb, Brother Fire and Sister Water, for the whole of creation is a brotherhood with a common loving Father, in whose embrace all were created from the beginning.'

"'I don't want to belittle the Franciscan vision,' I said, 'but surely others, both before and after Francis, have had similar visions, even if they have not been expressed in such a poetic way?'

"'Oh yes,' said Tony, 'but I'm only just beginning. The vision of Francis didn't end there. He wasn't just a romantic dreamer, but a practical realist, who could see into others because he had already learned to see into himself, and what he saw was that although all men may well be brothers and sisters to one another, that didn't necessarily make them into a loving, caring brotherhood. You may well put people into a building and call it a friary, you may call the inhabitants of that friary brothers, but that does not make them into a brotherhood. It doesn't make them into anything more than a brotherhood in name, unless something further happens to breathe into them the brotherly love that makes them into a genuine family.

"'What Francis and his followers wanted to do was not just to inspire men with a vision of a brotherhood into which they were born, but with a brotherly love by which they could live together in harmony and peace. The way he decided to do this resulted in a revolutionary kind of religious life that had never been known before.'

"'And what was it?' I asked eagerly.

"'It was very simple really. It was to live the Gospel life to the letter, and to follow in the footprints of Jesus Christ.'

"'But surely that wasn't new?' I said. 'Don't you think all the other Orders founded centuries before Francis were trying to do this? Don't you think it's a bit of a cheek to suggest that this was unique to Francis and his followers? Didn't all the Orders before Francis base themselves on the Gospels?"

"'Oh yes. In general on the Gospels," said Tony, "but not on the Gospel lifestyle. Let me explain what I mean for it's rather important if you are to understand Franciscan spirituality. In general, the religious life that pre-dated Francis was monasticism. All other movements, like the Canons Regular, who either grew out of or based themselves on the monastic life, never intended to base themselves on the Gospel lifestyle. Whether they followed the rule of Benedict, Basil or Augustine for that matter, they saw their origins in the lifestyle as lived by the early Christians immediately after the Resurrection, the lifestyle described in Chapter Two of the Acts of the Apostles. Monasticism was seen as a development of that lifestyle, and any monastic reform always looks back to the first Christian community, to rediscover the principles on which its own lifestyle was based, and upon which it must always renew itself.

"'Now Francis wasn't a great religious thinker. He wasn't a great theologian or intellectual for that matter, so when he realized God was calling him to go into the towns and the villages, into the market-places as well as the churches with the message of the Gospel, he knew that there could only be one lifestyle for him and his followers. That was the lifestyle as lived by Jesus with his disciples during the public ministry.

"'Strange though it may seem, no religious life had done that before Francis, and some, like the Benedictines, positively excluded it with their vow of 'stability.' What I'm saying is in no way a criticism of monasticism, because the monastic life was never founded to evangelize the world through apostolic work, but through contemplative prayer.

"'But what about those evangelical movements that, like Francis, were inspired by the Crusaders and traveled around preaching the Gospels and living in poverty?" I said.

"'They all claimed to live the apostolic lifestyle," said Tony. "A style of life based on that of the first apostles, who spread the good news all over the known world of their day. Nowhere in the writings of Francis does he use the phrase 'the apostolic lifestyle.' He and his brothers bound themselves to live the lifestyle that Jesus and His disciples lived before the Resurrection. Now Francis saw that there were three inseparable ingredients in this way of life.

"It is an eremitical or solitary life, a community life, and an apostolic life. All three are so inseparably bound together that no authentic Franciscan life can exist if one element is permanently lacking. Now this is the lifestyle Francis chose for himself and his followers as the spiritual structure that would enable them to live a life of continual conversion of heart. This continual conversion of heart would so open them to the brotherly love of God, the Holy Spirit, that they would be bonded into a loving, caring brotherhood, that would preach their message to the world before ever they opened their mouths. This is why the first friars introduced themselves as penitents from Assisi, whose first work was to practice the repentance that they would preach to others. Like their Father Francis they would imitate Jesus by retiring repeatedly into solitude, to practice the inner repentance of heart that would enable them to receive something of the fullness of life that they would then share with their brothers in community. Only in this way could they be perfectly one, and so embody the prayer made by Jesus at the Last Supper, so that they could be a sign to the world of the brotherhood they wanted to extend to all.

"'Knowing that all this would be impossible without the brotherly love of God, Francis wanted it written into his rule that the real General of his Order was the Holy Spirit, but the final draft had been drawn up before he could do what he had planned.

"'After the death of Francis many of his followers became so entangled in disputes about interpretation of the rule, the size of the houses they lived in, or the meaning of the poverty they professed, that they gradually forgot to go to the cave, to the hermitage where Francis's great vision was first seen in darkness and sustained in an ongoing purification that ever widened and deepened the spiritual horizon that he saw so clearly.

"'The inevitable happened. Although the Christ-centered spirituality that he had re-enkindled was spread across the continents and down the centuries, it lost the breadth and depth that only the true mystic sees, and so a new spirituality emerged that spread all over Europe. This personal piety, full of feeling and sentiment, that made Jesus a friend and personal Savior, was not bad in itself, so long as it was a starting point, as it usually is anyway; but when it became an end in itself, it soon degenerated into the worst sort of pietism. It inevitably tended to emphasize a spiritual self-indulgence that turned a blind eye to the social needs of others, and to the brotherhood of all in God, which is the goal of all authentic Christian endeavor.

"'It was not surprising that many right-minded Christians became tired of this personal, individualistic piety that soon began to prevail, and were inspired by the new ideas and ideals of the ancient world that soon began to inspire the whole of Europe. No one could say that the manly, no-nonsense, moral teaching of Socrates was over-sentimental, or closed to the needs and necessities of one's fellow man. Who could blame genuine Christians for being inspired by this high and noble vision for humanity? What then was lost to view as the vision of Francis faded, seemed to rise up anew in the vision of Socrates, but it was doomed to failure because it depended solely on the endeavor of Man.

"'It was not surprising then that the new emphasis on man-power that so deeply affected Christian theology after the Renaissance heralded a spirituality that made Jesus look far more like a great moral teacher than a mystic. He tended to become a model for men and women bent upon changing themselves, and the world around them by a self-generated man-power that banished the power of God or the Holy Spirit to the outer boundaries of Christian spirituality where He has remained ever since.

"'Only yesterday I was searching the library for books on the Holy Spirit and found only three. They were entitled *The Forgotten God*, *The Lost Paraclete* and *The Unknown God*. It is not surprising that the religious life that has prevailed for the last four hundred years or more has lost a true sense of community, for without a theology of the Holy Spirit there will be no theology of community life. Instead, religious foundations have tended to become groupings of individuals sharing a common ideal, to bring about God's Kingdom in the world by the same intensive endeavor with which it is presumed they have changed themselves in the first place — and I don't exempt the Franciscan Order from being tarred with the same brush.

"'When I finished all my research into the context of Franciscan spirituality, I went back to my spiritual director and told him about my findings. He seemed genuinely impressed that I had been able to discover so much in such a short time. 'However,' he said, 'the proof of the pudding is in the eating. What you find in the library is not necessarily the same as you will find in the friary, so next holidays go to a friary and see for yourself.'

"'I came to East Bergholt and wasn't disappointed.'"

"'If I hadn't experienced the friendly fraternity and the brotherly love for myself during the past week," I said, "I don't think I would have fully understood all that you have been trying to say. But I have, and so I do; but it all seems a bit too good to be true. What was your novitiate like? Was the approach totally different from my experience?"

"'No, I'm afraid I can't say it was, but we didn't take it too seriously. I'm afraid it was based on the old-fashioned moralist approach that you had to endure. Looking back on it, it had nothing much to do with the Gospels or Franciscan spirituality for that matter, although paradoxically stories from the Franciscan sources were told ad nauseam to illustrate a Christian humanism that had little to do with Saint Francis but far more to do with the spirituality of the 'Enlightenment.'"

"'What makes you so hopeful about the future?" I said.

"'Well, the new biblical theology that is even now spreading like wildfire all over the Continent is just beginning to reach us. It's a back-to-the-Gospel spirituality that is evidently here to stay. What could be better news for Franciscans? I believe we are once again on the threshold of a new Franciscan spring, and so does everyone else here. That's one more reason why there's such a tremendous spirit among the students."

"'Well, Tony," I said, "I don't mind telling you you've inspired me with all that you've said. In fact I already think I have found here what I have been looking for, at least in part, though somehow I don't feel I want to join you. For some time now I've become more and more convinced that I want to pursue my spiritual journey alone as a layman, but I can't see any reason why I can't become a lay Franciscan if there is such a thing."

"'Of course there is. Don't forget Francis never became a priest and he founded a Third Order especially for people like you. Go and have a chat with Rufo about it. He's the expert on the Third Order."

"'Who?"

"'Father Rufino. He lectures in dogma and he's a very good man. Go and have a chat with him. I'll arrange it for you if you like."

"'Thanks," I said. "Quite apart from anything else I could do with going to confession."

'I was sitting on a bench in the garden, thinking over all Tony had said, while I waited for the time Tony had arranged for me to go and see Father Rufino. I had never seen Tony, or Samuel as he was now called, so enthusiastic about anything before.

'What a pity that so many of Tony's dreams faded, as the support and brotherly love that he experienced during his student days at East Bergholt waned with the years, and finally seemed to let him down in South Africa, where he worked as a missionary until the late 60's. Somehow his dream of extending the great vision of Francis to a country stricken with the insidious disease of apartheid wasn't shared by all his fellow missionaries, or at least the practice was pitted with too many compromises for him to accept.

'As he felt the support of his fellows failing, at least in what he thought mattered most, he sought it elsewhere and found it in a new form of life that changed the whole direction of his spiritual journey. But that's another story that he has told in his own book *Love with No Regrets.*

'I was so lost in my own thoughts that I hadn't noticed a young and extremely attractive nun who'd apparently been walking around the garden for some time, until she suddenly perched herself rather uneasily at the far side of the bench that I was sitting on.

'"You must be Sammy's brother," she said, rather coyly.

'"Yes, I've come to spend Christmas with him."

'"We call him Gregory Peck," she said. "He's the heartthrob of the convent, and beyond. When it's his turn to serve on the altar, all the girls from the village flock to swoon over his every move. You're not bad-looking yourself. Are there any more handsome young men in your family?"

'"I have a younger brother, David," I said, "but he's still at school."

'"And you're studying in gay Paree, I hear," she said, shuffling a little closer to me on the bench. "I know what young men get up to in Paree, so there's no need to be shy with me."

'I felt more and more uncomfortable, as she moved far too close for comfort.

'"Did you see the poster on Liverpool Street Station on your way down?" she asked.

'"No," I admitted.

'"Pity," she said. "You'd have laughed if you did, because some naughty little boy had written something rude underneath it."

'"Oh, really."

'"Shall I tell you what it was?"

'"You can if you like," I said, though I was beginning to feel distinctly uncomfortable. No nun had ever spoken like this before.

'"Well, it said *Harwich for the Continent,* and underneath was written *and Paris for the incontinent!*'

'I blushed slightly, but managed a pathetic little laugh to hide my confusion rather than to share the joke. And then, would you believe it, she looked me straight in the face and said, "Are you continent, Peter?"

'I turned scarlet and simply didn't know what to do or what to say, and then things went too far. She put her arm around me and said, "If I come to Paree, Peter, will you show me the night life? Take me to the Moulin Rouge and the Folies Bergeres?"

'As she made as if to kiss me, I sprang to my feet and burst out in a loud voice, "I'm going to confession."

'As I turned round to go into the house I was horrified to see that almost every window in the friary was open, and all three floors seemed to be full of faces looking down upon me, and the squalid little scene that had just been played out in the garden. It was like one of those terrible nightmares when you are caught up in a compromising and embarrassing situation, and you are just beginning to thank your lucky stars that no one will ever know about it when a curtain sweeps back, lights are turned up, and a spotlight beams in to highlight your humiliating circumstances.

'I took one look at the audience and then glanced back to see the seductive little Sister laughing convulsively in a deep baritone voice, that instantly betrayed the practical joke that made me the laughing stock of the community.

'Father Rufino was a fascinating character — small, round and dumpy, with a God-given tonsure that looked as if it had been painted on him by some irreverent cartoonist. If the Order had only had the foresight to patent him before the salt and pepper-pot designers had copied him they'd have made a fortune. But despite his rather comic appearance he wasn't particularly amused by the antics of the students. It wasn't that he lacked a sense of humor, far from it, but he thought that they ought to behave with a little more sensitivity to the feelings of visitors, and save their practical jokes for themselves. His concern for my feelings and his obvious sense of compassion touched me, and Tony's obvious reverence for him made me determined to explain myself to him as fully as possible, and to ask him to guide me forward in the direction that I myself could not see clearly.

'"I'm afraid that's one thing I can't do," said Father Rufino. "People always want me to tell them where to go and how to get there, and the truth of the matter is I simply don't know. I had a letter this morning that is typical from a congregation of Sisters, who want me to come and talk at their chapter, to tell them what they must do, and in what direction they should be going. My reply is always the same. 'I don't know, but I know Someone who does.'

"'I believe that we are at a critical point in the Church's history, and it's the time not so much for doing but for being; for being totally and radically open to the Truth, or we will never know where we should be going, never mind how we should be getting there. My reply to you then is exactly the same as I will give to them.

"'Try to restructure your daily lifestyle in such a way that you have time each day to allow the Truth-giving Spirit in — then as Jesus promised at the Last Supper He will make all things known to you. The experience you had in Notre Dame was undoubtedly authentic. It was the genuine touch of God. I have no doubt about it. Saint Francis had a similar experience that was the moment of truth in his life. He had been dilly-dallying for far too long when, late one evening when he was singing his way home with his drinking pals, he suddenly experienced the touch of God as you did, and it gave him the strength to do what he'd been putting off for many months.

"'He spent almost three years in solitude, living the life of a hermit. This was when he first learned how to repent in prayer, so that the spirit of truth could gradually enter more fully into him, to show him what he must do, and give him the power to do it.

"'There's no such thing as instant sanctity, as Francis had to find out for himself the hard way. I believe in everything from instant coffee to instant resurrection, but instant sanctity — I'm afraid there is no such thing, and never let anyone tell you otherwise. I'm prepared to believe in instant conversion, instant emotion, instant tongues, instant healing, instant miracles if there is evidence, oh yes! But instant sanctity — oh no! Never be deceived, Peter.

"'Sanctity is a gradual process that is God's work. It is only brought to completion in years if a person believes firmly enough to persevere in prayer beyond the first emotional beginnings into the prayer of naked faith, when they have to journey on, practicing the repentance that teaches them how to turn repeatedly and open themselves to God, even though they feel as if they are talking to a brick wall.

"'To persevere in that sort of prayer is the certain way to sanctity, as you must learn for yourself — then you are open to the action of God as never before. When He gets inside you it is with a love that will empty you of all other loves that prevent you from making the total surrender to Him, that will enable you to become His perfect instrument. This is what Francis had to learn, but it's a hard lesson because it means experiencing a radical inner purification through which the power of the 'Old Man' is prayed out of you by the only true exorcist, the Holy Spirit.

"'Yes, prayer beyond first beginnings is a real exorcism. That's why it is so painful, and that's why so many people who start so well end up by running away from it, and that's why there are so few saints. Francis didn't run away, but the experience was so grueling that at the end of several months of this purifying prayer people hardly recognized him for the bright and breezy young man who went into solitude in the first place.

"'I'm telling you this, Peter, because you, too, have been touched by God; you, too, have been called to journey into the desert of prayer where the oases are few and far between, and I want to encourage you by fortifying you with the truth, so as to help you to persevere when all seems purposeless. It was in his solitary prayer that Francis was gradually purified and prepared to see what God wanted him to do, though he did not see it for several years. Then, when the first stage of his spiritual journey was over, he was open and sensitive to hear the voice of God, that his old soiled self could not hear before.

"'It was in a little church hidden in the woods, dedicated to Saint Mary of the Angels, that he participated in the mystery of the Mass as never before. The words of the Gospel struck him like lightning, and like lightning they set him afire to do the word he had heard. The command was simple. 'Go out in poverty to preach the Gospel of God's Kingdom of peace to all.'

"'Now like a bolt from the blue he saw what he must do, but the sacred mysteries that showed him what he must do also gave him the power to do it. Whenever the power of God's Spirit is unleashed, it touches the heart and the head at the same time. Francis had been to many Masses before, but never before had the power that was unleashed within them had such a devastating effect, as it did that February day in 1208 on the Feast of Saint Matthias.

"'You must do what Francis did, Peter. Follow the call that you have already received. Neither I nor anyone else can tell you more than that, except how to persevere, because it will be in and through your patient perseverance that the Spirit of God will touch you further in His good time to enable you to see, as Francis saw, what you must do, and at the same time give you the power to do it." Father Rufino paused for a moment to fill a large brier pipe with Saint Bruno from his tobacco pouch. It gave me the opportunity to ask a question I'd meant to ask Tony.

"'As an outsider to Franciscan spirituality, at least until today, I'd always associated poverty with Saint Francis, but I'm not quite sure why it was so important to him?"

"'Well," said Father Rufino, "it's a big subject that I can't go into in any detail now but let me just say this. Francis wanted to be poor because Brother Jesus, the One in whose footprints he wanted to tread, was poor. He could not get over the fact that the One with other-worldly wealth beyond imagining freely chose to give it all up to become poor as a naked and helpless baby in a wooden crib, just in order to become our brother. And, furthermore, He allowed Himself to be stripped naked, and hammered to a wooden cross as a helpless man, to speak to all men of every time and every age of a timeless, ageless love that burned in Him, for all. But this was not the ultimate in poverty for Francis. The ultimate in poverty was that when that helpless man was raised by and into the fullness of God's love and was seated at His right hand, love still continued to compel Him to abase Himself as common bread and wine, to enter into us whenever we choose to receive Him.

"'This is why nobody will ever understand Francis or Franciscan spirituality until they can realize just how important the Mass was to Francis himself and to all who followed him. It is a subject that he returns to again and again in his writings.

"'The Mass is the sacrament or sign for Francis of the continual outpouring of love that will alone enable a person to enter fully into Brother Jesus.

"'Francis did not take part in the holy mystery with the frequency that is commonplace today, for in his day reverence was shown more by the quality of the inner disposition of heart with which one approached the sacred table. This is why the whole of Francis's life was punctuated by protracted periods of solitude, so that in silence he could savor, and assimilate, the grace poured out in the sacred mysteries. He saw so clearly that without time set aside for this solitary assimilation then the Mass would be fruitless, not in itself but in himself. You see Love can't be forced on anyone — not even God's Love, because forced love is a contradiction in terms. So if a person does not create space and time to allow that love into them then that love can't possibly touch them, never mind change them. Anyone who thinks that merely going to Mass no matter how often changes them without putting aside set time to receive the graces poured out in the Mass is treating the Mass as magic. Francis saw so clearly that personal prayer is the time we freely choose to set aside, to digest and assimilate, to interiorize the personal love of God available at all times to the person who's got time, for what time was made for in the first place.

"'I often stay with a small community of sisters who live in a little house not far from here, from which they engage in various forms of social apostolate. Every day the main concern seems to be how to 'get their Mass in.' They have no resident chaplain and so they have to go out to different places, depending on the demands made by their work-load. The strange thing is that though they'd never think of missing their Mass, and would have terrible feelings of guilt if they did, they could nevertheless go for months without a solid block of time for personal prayer, and they wouldn't have the slightest twinge of conscience. The Mass does not automatically dispense grace — it's not a magic rite.

"'Christianity is an end to magic. It inaugurates a new age. It is the age of love. Its message is simple: human beings are not saved by magic but by love. Now loving must be learned, and prayer is the place where that learning process takes place, in such a way that the love of God is able to enter into human loving gradually bringing it to perfection.

"'So it's pointless to keep celebrating the Sacrament that is signifying the outpouring of love, without setting aside the time after that Sacrament to assimilate, to digest, to interiorize that personal love of God through a process of interior repentance of heart.

"'I find it quite frightening when I see so many contemporary priests and religious endlessly getting worked up and excited by experiments with all sorts of new ways of presenting the Sacrament in a modern way without at the same time seeing that their 'performances' are pointless unless they point the participators to personal prayer. Too many still think that personal prayer is an optional extra for the extraordinarily pious, for the young, for the novices passing through their first fervor, or for the aged, who are too old for apostolic work, but is a luxury that simply cannot be afforded by the busy man-about-town religious of today, who has got the whole world to change by their intensive missionary endeavor. If they can't afford time for prayer, they won't be able to give love to others, because they will be spiritually bankrupt themselves.

"'If you're merely content to get your Mass in each day, and say your prayers of obligation, before rushing out to change the world, then it's the red light, and if you regularly ignore the red light then spiritual disaster is inevitable."

'I was just beginning to get a little embarrassed as the preacher in Father Rufino was getting quite worked up about a matter that was obviously close to his heart.

"'Forgive me." he said, "but I do feel so strongly about these matters I'm afraid I do get worked up."

"'Please don't apologize, Father. I do see what you mean. In fact, I see what you mean more clearly than I have seen it before."

"'You see," said Father Rufino, "there will never be an effective apostolate outside of prayer unless that apostolate is transformed by a Christ-like selflessness that has first to be learned inside of prayer. Don't be deceived by a lot of pretentious gobbledygook that is peddled today by the purveyors of a so-called 'apostolic spirituality,' who talk of contemplation in action in such a sophisticated way, that the undiscerning hardly notice that it's just another way of conning the overworked and the undernourished into believing that they are mystics in the market-place.

"'There has never been a mystic in the market-place, who hasn't first learned in the desert-place to die to the old self-centered egotist within. If the lesson is not first learned there, then the would-be apostle will only shape their apostolate in the so-called market-place to suit their own needs and promote their own honor and glory, though they'll kid themselves it's for God's.

"'Now the selflessness that is practiced inside of prayer must be put into practice outside of prayer, so that it suffuses everything we do. Inside of prayer a person may use the rosary, a meditation, the slow meditative reading of the Scriptures or some other means to help them keep turning their hearts to God. Outside of prayer they may use teaching techniques, counseling skills, or medical expertise, and in doing this they are in fact practicing the repentance of all times. Or, if you like, the prayer of all times, what Our Lord calls the prayer without ceasing. The prayer without ceasing is simply the continual dying of the disciple to their old self as they try to live for God, and the neighbor in need. Gradually they come to learn through faith, and eventually even through feeling, that in the Dying is the Rising, as every moment of death to the 'Old Man' is a moment when the life of the 'New Man' rises within them.

"'The dying done in this daily prayer without ceasing is the only acceptable offering that is made when they next take part in the sacred mysteries. This is the offering that unites them with the offering made by Jesus, and it opens them to the resurrection life that He received without measure on the first Easter Day. So in a lifetime of dying through daily trying the believer is progressively opened ever more fully to the life that will alone fashion them into the person they have committed themselves to follow.

'"Now let's see how the process that I have been trying to explain is worked out in the life of Jesus Himself. It can be seen most clearly at the final moments of His life on earth, although it took place at every moment of that life. When He knew that His hour had finally come, He knew the terrible ordeal that He would have to endure at the hands of those who wished to destroy Him. He felt afraid, He felt insecure, He felt in need of support and of strength; after all, He was human. He therefore called upon those whom He loved most in this world for their support, told them to prepare a meal that would reaffirm their mutual love, which would at the same time provide the opportunity for all of them to receive the help of the Father, whose strength and support He needed most of all.

'"The Sacrament celebrated at the Last Supper unleashed in an unprecedented way the fullness of love that Jesus would receive in an unrestricted and abiding way the following day, to give Him the strength to face that day with unlimited courage and fortitude. Once the Sacrament had been celebrated He went into the Garden of Gethsemane to assimilate and digest the love that He had received, to personalize it in deep interior prayer.

'"The angel of consolation symbolized the help and the strength given through the dying He had to do, in trying to surrender to His Father's will, amid blood, sweat and tears. That help and strength filled His heart with the otherworldly power and energy that overflowed into every part of His body, so that the will of the Father could be done, not just with His heart but with every part of His human personality.

'"Now He could stand with poise and dignity before Annas

and Caiaphas, and discuss the nature of authority and kingship with Pilate when He was half flayed alive. Even on the road to His death He found time to stop and sympathize with the women of Jerusalem, to forgive the soldiers, who battened His hands to the cross, and promise the good thief the same Paradise to which He Himself was going.

'"When the last act of surrender was made it was a sacrifice made with the whole of His human personality from the depths of His dark and depressed mind, to the cut and bleeding body, it was an act that had been rehearsed time and time again throughout His life in His repentance without ceasing, His prayer without ceasing. The moment the final surrender was made was the moment when the life He had received in part was given in full measure, to overflow to eternity on all who would follow Him. Any believer who would follow Christ must learn to undergo all that He underwent, and experience all He experienced, even though their match-wood crosses may seem at times more than they can bear. This is the only way to the transformation and the transfiguration that is everyone's deepest desire.

'"True imitation of Christ then, means not firstly copying His outer behavior but the way in which He endeavored to turn, open, and surrender Himself to the Father with His heart, His mind, and with His whole personality. This is the only way we will be able to welcome into our hearts the self-same spirit that animated Him, so that everything can be done to death in us that prevents the perfect love of God, and the perfect love of neighbor being embodied in all we say and all we do.

'"The inner peace and joy that is experienced as the human harmony of spirit lost by sin is restored, is the psychological expression of the in-dwelling promised by Christ Himself to the perfect disciple, whose very body gradually becomes the place where the Father and the Son and the Holy Spirit make their home on earth."

'Before I left Father Rufino, he said, "Don't think that because you have been impressed by what I have said you must become a Franciscan. No, it means that you must become a better Christian. Francis is only the example I have used because he is such a good one."

'I spent the rest of my Christmas holidays with my parents at East Didsbury, a suburb of Manchester where I was born and where I had grown up. My parents were so pleased to see me — it was the first time that they had spent their Christmas without their three sons, for David had spent his Christmas in Paris with his friend Bernard. I was sorry that I had been so thoughtless, for I could easily have spent Christmas with them before visiting Tony. My mother thought I was beginning to use home as a convenient hotel, and I think she was right. I can't help but smile as I look back, because with all my traveling and with all the different places I went to and the different people I met in search of spiritual meaning, it was finally at home, and from my parents, that I learned more about the spiritual life and the mystic way than from any other single person. That's another story, however, that will have to be told elsewhere.

'Despite what Father Rufino had said, I was now quite clear in my own mind that I wanted Saint Francis to be the hand that would point me on the way to follow in the footprints of Jesus. I prayed every day that God would show me how I, as a layman, could follow that way.

'Only four days before I was due to return to Paris that prayer was answered although I didn't fully realize it at the time. It all began with a letter from Madame de Gaye, the lady with whom my brother David had been staying in Paris.

'David had apparently told her of my rather dismal lodgings at Place Pigalle, made even more dismal by the departure of my friend Boris. She was quite adamant that I should stay with her at Rue de Magdebourg for the remainder of my final year at the Sorbonne. The letter was providential and my immediate acceptance turned out to be one of the major turning points in my life.'

* * * * * * * * *

You can have too much of a good thing and I think I'd had too much religion for one day, so I lay on my bed unable to sleep as my mind went on and on, turning over and over as it failed to digest the over-rich mixture of spiritual nourishment with which I had indulged myself.

I picked up a book on the Highland clearances to help settle my mind so that I could sleep a little more easily. It not only sent me to sleep but into the most terrible nightmare that I have ever experienced; a nightmare that woke me up in the early hours of the following morning to experience something even worse.

I could hear the **6** banging on the door. I
could hear the constables trying to shoulder their way into the
cottage. There was the sound of children screaming — my children;
and a woman, my wife, shouting at me from the bedside.

"It's Beatson and his men. Quick, wake up for God's sake!"

In a flash I'd summed up the situation. I turned over and
pretended not to hear. I knew who I was supposed to be, and
how I was expected to act. In the strange world of dreamland you
can be two people at one and the same time without any apparent
contradiction. Although I knew I was supposed to be the brave
Angus MacNeil, the champion wrestler, who was expected to leap
out of bed and take on the posse of policemen single-handed, I
knew that underneath it all it was still me, the cowardly James
Robertson, who just didn't want to know. Even if I did my body
couldn't move. I was paralyzed with fear, and sweating like a pig
waiting for the slaughterhouse to open.

I was still pretending to be fast asleep, as I heard the door
give way and the men rush into the room to drag me and my family
off to the transporter. To my shame, I flung myself out of bed on
to my knees, screaming at the intruders, "Mercy, mercy, please
don't hit me. I'll come quietly, but please don't hit me for God's
sake."

There I was, in a state of semi-hysteria, kneeling on the floor
in front of a group of half a dozen men, shaking half with fear at
the thought of what they might do to me, and half with shame
that my wife should see her man reduced to a cringing, blubbering

coward. I must have been hysterical for I suddenly felt two mighty smacks across my face that brought me to my senses, and I woke up panting with exhaustion to see that thankfully there was no wife to witness my humiliation, no children to see their father groveling on the floor, and begging for mercy before the men he should have been hurling from his hearth and home.

But the men were there, sure enough, and this time I wasn't dreaming.

"Get up and sit down," said a tough but cultured voice from somewhere behind a battery of powerful torches that were shining into my eyes.

Before I knew what had happened, I was being interrogated by two men who stood out in front of the group. They wanted to know who I was, and what I was doing, but it was evident that they had been almost as surprised to see me as I was to see them.

From the questions that followed it became clear they were more interested in Peter than they were in me. I had to tell them the whole story of his tragic death at sea, and then before they were satisfied I had to prove he had existed in the first place by showing them his birth certificate and medical card. Everything I said was taken down in detail.

By the time they were ready to go, I had sufficiently recovered my composure to ask them who they were, and what right they had to burst into someone else's house in the middle of the night.

One of the men who had been doing most of the talking said that they were searching for a gang of drug smugglers, who they believed were operating in the Isles, dropping their cargo at night from a light aircraft on one of the uninhabited islands.

It was about four o'clock in the morning when I saw the small launch that had brought them reach what looked like a Royal Navy mine-sweeper about a mile away from Calvay. It took me a couple of hours to regain my composure, to get over the shock of the nightmare that had come true, and it took me another hour to assess what had happened.

It didn't add up. They were not looking for drug smugglers. That was evidently a trumped up story to hide the real reason for their visit. If they were really looking for drug smugglers, why hadn't they questioned me more thoroughly? When I said I was a friend of Peter's and had come to sort out his affairs, they hadn't questioned me further. No, it wasn't me that interested them, nor was it any mythical drug smugglers, it was Peter, that was quite apparent to me. But why?

When Father James came over to visit me about the middle of the morning, I explained to him what had happened, but he had no more idea than I who my visitors had been.

"The whole thing is very mysterious," he said, "but you are right. It just doesn't add up. Did you get the name of the ship, by the way?" he said.

"Yes, I did. It was quite light and I used Peter's binoculars. It was H.M.S. Wasperon."

"Well, that's genuine enough," said Father James. "That was the ship used by the Navy to supply us with food last time we had a seamen's strike, but I have simply no idea what it is all about."

It took me until lunchtime to get over my humiliating little adventure. What on earth did those men think of me? Of the shabby, cowardly performance that I had put on when they entered the room? Thank God I had managed to hide my true identity, managed to hide the fact that I was a priest. That would have made things worse. At least, it would for me.

I spent the rest of the day trying to forget that squalid little scene that had been enacted in the small hours of that June morning by mechanically addressing dozens of letters to Peter's correspondents so that they could be informed about his death.

I had sufficiently recovered from my early morning ordeal by the evening to relax in front of a peat fire that I had made, more to cheer me up than to keep me warm. I settled down to read Peter's next typescript. It was entitled:

'Despite my immediate acceptance of Madame de Gaye's kind invitation, I nevertheless felt rather apprehensive when I arrived at Cinq Rue de Magdebourg, because I had been a little overawed on my last visit by the comparative splendor of their large third-floor apartment. The dinner that I had shared with the family had been to welcome my brother David on his first visit to Paris. Since then he'd stayed with them several times, and Bernard de Gaye had spent several holidays at my own home in Manchester, without giving the slightest hint that he'd noticed the social chasm that separated the two families.

'It was from David, who was still staying at the apartment when I arrived, that Madame de Gaye had heard about my plight. I was simply stunned when she explained that she was not just a member of the Secular Franciscans, but that she was the president of the Third Order in Paris. Since my last visit her husband had died and the three eldest children had left home, leaving only Bernard, herself, and three servants residing in the more than ample accommodation. Madame de Gaye was a small bird-like woman whose long curved eyebrows, hooked nose, and slightly receding chin gave her a distinctly hawkish appearance, though she behaved at all times with the manners of a dove, at least with her equals or those she chose to treat as such.

'Nevertheless, I had the uneasy feeling that the servants saw more of the hawk than the dove, especially those who'd served her in her prime.

'She'd taken to wearing dowdy dark suits since her husband died, with a preference for black, despite the protestations of her family.

'She already knew the general direction that my life was beginning to take, partly from David, and partly from a feminine intuition that when harnessed with a genuine human compassion never ceases to amaze the more prosaic members of the human species. She had already guessed that the poor man of Assisi was beginning to beckon me to embrace a new lifestyle, that would sustain me into the future that was as yet quite unknown to me.

'Madame de Gaye never asked me anything. She just took me up the narrow staircase that led to the servants' quarters and showed me into two rooms. One would serve as a bedroom and the other as a study.

'"This is the place for a Franciscan," she said, with a low whisper and a knowing look that seemed to say I know your little secret, young man, and it's safe with me until it's safe for the world.

'"Since Christmas I've had to ask two of the servants to leave for we only have a small family now. Robert is old and he has nowhere to go. As he has great difficulty with the stairs I have asked him to move into my eldest son's room. Patrick is married now and living in Toulon. This means that you will be entirely alone. You can have the whole of the servants' quarters to yourself, except this room which we will share."

'She opened the door at the end of the corridor that opened into a beautiful little chapel, complete with the blessed Sacrament, a privilege granted to her forebears by the infamous Cardinal Richelieu, for unspecified services rendered to King Louis XIII.

'I couldn't believe my luck, nor could David, who was himself already beginning to experience a certain pull that would eventually lead him into religious life. For the time being however he was still full of his lifelong ambition to become an opera singer, and still quite oblivious of the fact that an ability to keep on the note for more than two seconds at a time is usually mandatory for one aspiring to such heights. He carried a book around with him at all times entitled *The Message of Fatima*, and he was aching for the years to tick by to 1960 when the famous "Fatima secret" would be revealed, or so he thought!

'I had done quite a lot of thinking during the holidays, and one question kept bugging me — why was it that all that I had been learning about prayer, was so little understood by Christians in general, and by religious in particular.

'I had met many good men and women who'd left religious

life because they couldn't find the prayer-life that they were so desperately looking for. I discovered that my experience in the novitiate was not unique, but commonplace.

'The main thing seemed to be the work, that you were told is your prayer, whenever you questioned the continual rush and bustle.

'It wasn't that prayer was denied, it just seemed to be misunderstood, so that it was very difficult to get any sympathy or understanding when you were led into prayer beyond first beginnings. Why is prayer so misunderstood? It was a question that I put to Père Le Bec at our first meeting after the holidays.

'"I'm afraid the answer to that is rather long and complex. You see, before the modern world came to birth at the Renaissance, the prevailing experience of mediaeval man was one of awe and profound reverence before the All Holy and transcendent God. Spend an hour tomorrow morning in Notre Dame. Gaze at the vastness of the nave; let your heart rise with the tall Gothic pillars, to be lost in the fine traceries that merge in the vaulting. Breathe in the whole atmosphere of that hallowed place, and you will experience something of the spirit that pervaded the religious consciousness of pre-Renaissance man.

'"These great cathedrals perfectly embody to this day the two great religious truths that dominated man in the Middle Ages. The utter transcendent majesty of God and, in comparison, the smallness, the humility of Man, totally aware of his absolute dependence on his Maker.

'"I am not holding any brief for the spirituality of mediaeval Europe. I don't believe in golden ages, but I do believe that with all its faults the particular emphasis on man's weakness and dependence upon God, created as it always will the perfect inner dispositions of heart necessary for an authentic mystical prayer life to develop.

'"When you leave Notre Dame spend a couple of hours in the Louvre. Gaze at the building itself, its fine neoclassical architecture and the great works of the masters of the European

Renaissance. You will still experience awe, but this time your awe will not be directed so much to God but to Man, to his greatness, to his achievements. The master works of Gothic architecture cry out, 'look at Man, look at what he can do.'

"'Man's unquestioning belief in himself and in what he can achieve was the central dogma of Renaissance man and it began to seep deep down to saturate Christian spirituality. Its progress was suddenly speeded on its way and strengthened as the Church was forced into a reaction against the reformers, who proclaimed that good works were a waste of time.

"'The new religious Orders that sprang up everywhere, from the seventeenth century onwards, embodied in their activity-centered spiritualities the Church's answer to the reformer's insistence on the futility of good works. The new lands that were being discovered almost daily would be conquered for Christ. Ignorant and ailing Christendom would be re-educated and nurtured back to physical as well as spiritual health, and heresy-ridden Europe would be won back to the one true faith.

"'All this would be achieved by man's intensive apostolic endeavor, albeit with God's help, but the scales had been tilted in favor of Man and the balance has not yet been redressed. Another heresy that came this time from within the Church led to a further over-emphasis on man-power. It's called quietism and involved a complete misunderstanding of the classical mystical authors, by various groups of religious enthusiasts and voyagers, that led to all sorts of gross immorality. Its inevitable condemnation led to anti-mystical 'witch-hunts' throughout Christendom, led by people quite incapable of distinguishing authentic mystical prayer from the counterfeit.

"'Saint Teresa of Avila and Saint John of the Cross came under the cloud, and were openly condemned with anyone else who wrote about docility, pacifism or recollection in prayer. Work, work and more work was the best antidote to quietism. The effects of these 'witch-hunts' have remained with us to the present day.

"'It's interesting to notice that although the four centuries before the Council of Trent produced the greatest crop of front line mystical writers that Christendom has ever known, the four centuries after Trent have produced hardly any. Who is there between Saint John of the Cross and the present time who could be classed as an original mystical writer of the first order? Yet between Saint Bernard and Saint John of the Cross they are almost two a penny.

'"I don't want to give the impression that genuine spirituality stopped with the Council of Trent, or draw any ridiculous black and white conclusions about the last four centuries. These centuries have given the Church saints, martyrs, and men and women of extraordinary spiritual caliber, but only because, in spite of the prevailing attitude to the contrary, they became poor in spirit."

'Père Le Bec's explanation made a lot of sense, and it sent me back to my books to read for myself more about the history of the counter-reformation.

'At the end of January Bernard, David and I went out for a meal followed by a film to celebrate David's birthday and his imminent departure for the more mundane ambience of the Lancashire Riviera. If it hadn't been for the lightning reactions of Bernard, the outing would have ended up in total tragedy instead of the total embarrassment that no one's presence of mind could have avoided.

'The manager of the famous Ritz Hotel was a friend of Madame de Gaye, who insisted on forcing half a dozen cocktails on us before we sat down to lunch. Bernard insisted that the *vin ordinaire* was no more intoxicating than lemonade, and we both believed him. We drew the line, however, when a large bottle of claret arrived at the table with the manager's compliments — that is, until Bernard explained that to refuse it would be insulting in the extreme, and would lead to social repercussions out of all proportion to a slight drowsiness at the most, that could easily be slept off at the cinema, if needs must.

'We took Bernard at his word, quite unaware that his word was only as good as an Englishman's capacity to sustain French wine, especially when welcomed by half a dozen American cocktails, that were already lurking in the lining of our stomachs. Even then, the sumptuous cinema seating could have saved us had the film been anything other than a new release entitled "On the Waterfront," starring Marlon Brando. It was a tense dockland drama that had the French audience entranced as the plot began to unfold.

'I was just about to fall asleep when David got the giggles. The more I nudged him, the more he laughed. He thought I was sharing the joke with him instead of trying to shut him up. People were starting to look around and I was just beginning to get angry when I saw for myself what David was laughing at. It was the sedate little sub-titles used to translate the picturesque dockland slang that was simply too much for us. I say, for us, for my anger gave way to mirth the moment I saw what David had seen. We both convulsed into laughter as American at its most colorful was rendered by French at its most conservative.

'"OK. Canary. Git the hell outa here before I make yer sing through your ass," said the mobster.

'"*M'sieur, allez, s'il vous plait,*" said the French sub-title, and "Oh, no," said David as he convulsed yet again into a laughter that was bordering on the hysterical, but I could do no more to control him, for I could no longer control myself, as we both dissolved into an uncontrollable drunken duet that shamed poor Bernard, who was completely nonplussed. But nonplussed or not, he too was evicted with his fellow musketeers, as the manager instructed two heavies to dump us unceremoniously on the pavement.

'Even the mobster would have been hard put to it to equal the language of the manager, as he began to scream at us as we rolled over on the floor, quite helpless, shrieking with laughter. Fortunately for us, Bernard was stone sober, and still gazing in horror at the sight of his friends groveling around on the floor, when the gendarme came over to book us.

'Like a flash, Bernard opened his wallet and handed a card

to the officer. "I am the Marquis de Magdebourg," he said haughtily, "and I withdraw my charges. I thought they were insulting my honor and our country, but I see now they are just drunken animals from England."

'He bundled us both into a taxi and said to the driver, "Place Pigalle, Montmartre."

"'*Les cochons*, the pigs!" he said to the gendarme, as we drew away from the curb. "They have had their entrées in the bars, let them have their main course in the brothels."

'Embarrassing it may all have been, but if it hadn't been for Bernard we'd have spent at least one night in the cells, and many more nights trying to explain how two "Holy Joes" ended up in a drunken heap on the Champs Elysees at three o'clock in the afternoon.

'I continued to go to Père Le Bec to direct my prayer life, but with his blessing and encouragement I began to go to Père Claude de Bois, a Capuchin and the spiritual director of the Third Order of Saint Francis, to direct me in the Franciscan vocation I had now definitely decided to embrace. Père de Bois' parents were both academics, so it was no surprise at all when they bred another in their only son Claude, who was rapidly becoming a hybrid lecturing at Louvain.

'He was so fond of books that he started breeding them, with almost indecent regularity, until someone introduced him to people shortly before his fortieth birthday.

'It was then that he suddenly discovered he had a heart that enabled him to read people with even greater understanding than his precious books. The cold and distant Polar Bear, as his students had called him, gradually changed and became a warm and cosy Teddy Bear, to whom everybody began to turn with their spiritual needs. He was a personal friend of Père Le Bec's, and I had without realizing it been introduced to him the previous year, at the day of recollection for priests given by Archbishop Arnou. I was embarrassed that he seemed to remember me when I had no recollection of meeting him.

'My decision to become a lay Franciscan was accompanied by all the usual hallmarks that invariably characterize conversion, including an insatiable desire to make a dramatic new start to my life. I was impatient to attain the sanctity that I read about with such enthusiasm in the lives of the saints. I wanted to make all-night vigils, fast and take upon myself all sorts of rigorous forms of asceticism that I had read about in the lives of people whose lives I wished to emulate, but Père Claude would have none of it.

'"Peter, you have much to learn, and the quickest way to learn is to be obedient to me in the lifestyle that you must adopt. This is the safest way to avoid the pride that will ruin you, and all your best intentions. The best antidote to pride is moderation as all the saints, including Saint Francis, taught to their followers."

'"But don't you think there is place for penance and mortification in the spiritual life?" I said, rather aggrieved that my plans had been thwarted.

'"Indeed I do," said Père Claude. "It's just that there are different forms of mortification. Some more appropriate for those still enjoying the flesh-pots of Egypt. Some more appropriate for those traveling in the desert, and some more appropriate for those camped by the oasis, or for those finally settled in the promised land.

"When a beginner is passing through his first fervor, everything seems easy. Prayer is full of sweetness and light, and so it is often helpful to impose some physical mortification with moderation, such as fasting, so that their empty stomachs can remind their arrogant minds of their human weakness, that their early success in prayer can easily make them forget. When a person is languishing in a spiritual desert, as you will soon find out for yourself, there's more than enough dying to be done without insisting on further self-imposed mortifications that can easily break the camel's back long before the next oasis comes into view.

'"When the spiritual traveler finally comes to settle in the promised land, he has such an abundance of everything that he desires, that he must needs express his gratitude in the language of true love which is sacrifice. Beginners always make the mistake of trying to copy the great ascetical practices of the saints: their heroic virtue, their self-denial, their almost super-human love towards others, without realizing that all this is but the outward expression of a love that fires them from within.

"'When I first read about the desert fathers in my novitiate, I started wearing a hair shirt that I made for myself. Every other night I kept vigil in the chapel, and fasted three times a week, only to end up in the sick-bay a near nervous wreck. With love all things are possible; without it, nothing is possible. I thought it was love that moved me, and it was, but unfortunately it was only self-love that made me think I could do for myself what only God can do. I was trying to copy the outward behavior of the saints, when I should have been exposing my heart to receive the same love that made such heroic behavior possible.'

"'I see what you mean, but what form of mortification should I practice? I feel I must do something,' I said.

"'All right, Peter, I'll impose a strict asceticism upon you; to begin with you will think it's too easy, but to end with you'll think it's far too hard.

"'Here is the principle. Don't give up anything you like or enjoy, save sin — except in so far as it prevents you from having consistent quality time each day for prayer, for it is there that you will learn how to open your heart to the love that will eventually enable you to do all, and everything, that is quite impossible without it. Don't let your youthful enthusiasm kid you into believing that it is all too easy. When love begins to purify the dross that is within you, you'll suddenly find that it is all too difficult.

"'Now, before I go any further, do you see the point of the principle, Peter?'

"'Yes, indeed I do, because I have seen it at work in a member of my own family only a few years ago. A cousin of mine had been given up as beyond redemption because he was an alcoholic, a drug addict and an inveterate gambler all rolled into one. All human reason, all appeals to his better nature, had failed to change him until a chance meeting with his future wife enabled a love to shaft into his heart that gave him the inner strength to give up everything that would have been quite impossible without it. There's no doubt about it, he was redeemed from what we thought was certain death by pure love, and if what Saint John said is true, it wasn't purely human love either."

"'How right you are," said Père Claude. "Your story perfectly makes the point. I couldn't have made it better. From now on you must give consistent daily time for prayer of the heart, so that the heart of God can communicate to your heart the stuff that the saints are made of. Anything and everything that prevents you from doing this must go out of your life — but no heroics please, because you are not capable of them. Just keep practicing the asceticism of the heart by setting aside each day consistent time for prayer, come what may, whether you feel like it or whether you don't.

"'Now, before you go, I would like to qualify this first principle with a second principle, which is this. You must not only practice the asceticism that demands *consistent* time for prayer each day, but you must also practice the asceticism that demands *quality* time for prayer each day — otherwise no matter how faithful you may be to begin with, you will not be able to remain consistent for long. To make my point, let us imagine that you endeavor to have thirty minutes set aside for prayer each day. Now, to make that time quality time you will need time set aside for preparation for prayer. You can't love someone unless you know them, so you need time for spiritual reading too, most especially the Gospels which Francis knew almost by heart. Furthermore, you need to seek out an environment in which you can have some silence and solitude, or that time for prayer will not be quality time.

"'Look at the life of Jesus that Francis tried to copy in his own life and you will see He not only sought out physical time for prayer but quality time, too. That's why He repeatedly went off alone into the desert, into lonely places where He could have the solitude that He needed. It was humility that led Him there, the humility that made Him realize that without the love that only

His Father could give Him, He would have nothing to give those He had come to serve.

"'Jesus not only left the madding crowd for solitary places but for rest and relaxation, too, and He took His disciples with Him.

"'You see, wet lettuces don't pray very well, so if you end up like a wet lettuce at the end of your day, you won't have quality time for prayer either. We are human beings, not automatons, and human beings need to have time for rest and relaxation. It's not a luxury, it's a necessity without which no prayer life will get off the ground. Don't think that because I criticize the work-madness that dominates religious people today that I am against work, far from it. Saint Paul said if a person does not work, neither should they eat, and Saint Francis said Amen to that. He was not ashamed to work with his own bare hands, he was proud of it, and he told his brothers to work, too, for the bread that they ate. It was only when there wasn't any that he told them to beg.

"'If a person thinks that they can drift around all day doing nothing but what their feelings fancy, then they won't have quality time for prayer at the end of the day, for if they have dissipated their work time, they will dissipate their prayer time also. So you see, Peter, having quality time for prayer means having time for spiritual reading, and time for rest and relaxation too, in an atmosphere of silence and solitude. At the moment your main work is the study that will enable you to serve others in the future, as it must help you to serve God now. If you don't take it seriously, then you won't be able to take your prayer seriously either, and before you know where you are you'll be everywhere but where you should be when it's time for prayer.

"'The whole of the spiritual life consists in trying to balance time for prayer and time for work, with time for rest and relaxation. It is such a delicate balance but everything depends on it. Get one out of proportion and you get everything out of proportion, and so you get nowhere in a hurry.

"'When I was a school-boy I was trying to break the school

record at what was then called the hop, step and jump. I think it's called the triple jump today. I simply got nowhere till I swallowed my pride and asked the school coach to come and tell me where I was going wrong. I was so eager to succeed that my hop was so long that I was totally off balance when it came to the step and the jump, and so I got nowhere. It was only when I learned to space out equally the hop, the step and the jump that I was finally able to break the record that I had set my heart on.

"'A young nursing Brother came to see me recently, who had been so convinced of the importance of prayer that he prayed for more than six hours a day with disastrous consequences. There was no time for rest and relaxation so he got more and more tense until his work began to suffer, and so did the people he was supposed to be serving. It took three months in a nursing home before he finally came to his senses, and saw he'd been ruled more by pride than by the prudence that should have guided him. But believe me, this is a very rare case for the main problem today is not that people give too much time for prayer, but too little. The activity-centered spiritualities that have predominated for too long hardly allow enough time for rest and relaxation, never mind for prayer. The key word then is balance, or what Archbishop Arnou calls Benedictine moderation. Bearing in mind what he said last year perhaps we could now define the essence of the spiritual life as gently trying to find the balance between prayer, rest and relaxation and work. If the balance ever comes, it will come as a gift from God, given to us, as we try to find it."

"'But what about the lives of the saints?" I said suddenly. "It seems to me that you often find a total lack of balance in their lives, even though they do preach moderation to others."

"'You are right,' said Père Claude. "That's because when the gift of moderation enables them to balance the different sections of their spiritual life in harmony, then they are totally open to the love of God at all times. When this happens, then these separate sections gradually begin to merge into one another in a new balance when, through love, everything is harmonized as one, at one and the same time, as it is in God, whose life they begin to reflect.

'"A saint may spend sixteen hours a day serving others and seem to have precious little time for prayer or relaxation, but that's only because through balance and moderation they allowed into their lives the sustaining and energizing love that makes every moment a moment which is totally open to God and to Man at one and the same time. I am now talking of the saint at the height of the spiritual life, not of the arrogant beginner who talks of contemplation in action as if they have scaled the heights when they're hardly in the foothills.

'"Well, Peter, that's all for now. You asked for asceticism and there you have it — the asceticism of the heart. Get that right, and everything else will fall into place. Remember the words of the Gospel. First seek God and His Kingdom, and then everything else will be given to you. If I had told you to give up drinking and smoking, to give up television and the cinema, and the opera that you so delight in, you would probably be quite happy, and happier still if I'd handed you a hair shirt and imposed fasting and vigils upon you, but it wouldn't last long. Like me, you would have ended up in the sick-bay, tired, exhausted and disillusioned. Remember the principle? — Don't give up anything you like or you enjoy unless it keeps you from consistent quality time for God each day in prayer. Then as His love begins to get inside you, and you begin to experience something of that love, something of the peace and joy that Jesus promised, then the paltry pleasures and pastimes, that meant so much to you before, will simply pale into insignificance as Someone else gradually becomes the center of your whole life and of your whole being, of all that you are, and of all that you say and do."

'It was a great disappointment to me when Père Claude was transferred to another friary in Lyon shortly before Easter. Although I still went to Père Le Bec, who helped me enormously with my prayer life, I could find no substitute for Père Claude to teach me the principles of Franciscan spirituality. Madame de Gaye did her best to make up for this, but she had to admit that she had neither the background nor the teaching ability to do more than encourage me to fend for myself as best I could, with the invaluable help of her library. I have never seen a better collection of books on Franciscan spirituality than at Cinq Rue de Magdebourg and I made full use of it when my studies allowed.

'Madame de Gaye may not have been a good teacher, but she was a good organizer, and she made full use of her gifts to plan the forthcoming year with a view to my profession into the Third Order of Saint Francis the following Easter. It was decided that we should both set off for Franciscan Italy the moment I received my examination results at the end of September. We would visit Assisi, and other places associated with Saint Francis, and then go to Clitunno to visit Madame's eldest daughter, Françoise, who had entered a Franciscan convent halfway between Spello and Spoleto.

'After that she had arranged for me to stay for four months at a Franciscan hermitage at Monte Casale, high up in the foothills of the Apennines, above Borgo San Sepolcro. She would then make her own way back to Paris where I would join her in the spring to make my final preparations for profession.

'Fortunately no repeats were necessary when my examination results came out, so I could journey to Italy at peace knowing that one particular chapter of my life had been completed, so enabling me to give my full attention to the next, although I had no idea as yet precisely how it was going to unfold.

'Madame de Gaye insisted on spending a full week in Florence so that she could take me to see the many great artistic masterpieces for which the city is so famous. She accepted that an unfortunate imbalance had come into Christian spirituality at the Renaissance, but she went out of her way to show me how mankind had benefited from the great movement in both the arts and the sciences. She admitted that she was no scientist but she could appreciate beauty, as could Saint Francis, who would surely have been captivated by the genius of God working through Man in the great artistic masters of the Renaissance.

'I have to admit that I was bowled over by the artistic splendors of Florence, but after three days I had had enough. I was standing in the church of La Santa Croce before Cimabue's breathtaking "Crucifixion," when I began to feel the pull to be alone; to go into solitude, not just because I ceased to savor what I saw, but because I wanted time to digest, and assimilate the goodness and beauty that reached out to me through the masterworks. I didn't want to go on looking at one copy after another. I wanted to gaze upon The Original.

'It is so good to have the sort of relationship with a person that enables you to express exactly how you feel and then to be understood.

'"I totally understand," said Madame de Gaye. "Now perhaps you will understand a little better why Francis kept feeling the urgent need to go into the darkness of the cave, to experience the source whose semblance he had seen in the light, then when he came out again he could see ever more clearly in all things around him, the One who is the All in all."

'Madame de Gaye made her point by taking me up to Fiesole and confining me to solitary prayer each day in the little Franciscan church high up on the hill, and then she exposed me at intervals to the fantastic vistas of the old town at carefully chosen moments of the day when the sun highlighted its beauty to best advantage. My heart literally leapt within me, not just because the physical and spiritual darkness of my solitary prayer contrasted so dramatically with what I saw in the light, but because I, too, was able to glimpse in some small way what Francis had seen in his darkness, so that I could see more clearly in the light what I had never seen before. It was a lesson that was learned well because the lesson was repeated again and again.

'As for the rest of our stay in Florence, and for the whole of our tour of Franciscan Italy, we never spent more than half the day outside the solitude to which we both continually returned. If we spent the mornings visiting towns, churches, and hermitages associated with Saint Francis, while drinking in the beauty of the

Italian countryside, then we would spend the afternoons or evenings savoring what we had seen, in solitary prayer. In this way we were able to follow in the footsteps of Saint Francis, not just because we followed the paths that he had followed, but because we were able to follow also the footprints that he had seen in the creation all about him, to the One who had made them in the first place.

'The only night that we stayed up late talking was on the night before we were to visit the convent where Madame de Gaye's eldest daughter, Françoise, was a Franciscan Sister. We were staying close by the convent at Campello sul Clitunno. It was the first time that Madame de Gaye had ever spoken at length about her family and about her daughter, Françoise. It seems that the de Gayes were, at least in their own eyes, impoverished French aristocrats, although in my eyes they seemed to be extremely wealthy.

'Bernard had only been exaggerating slightly when he claimed to be the Marquis de Magdebourg, for his grandfather was indeed a marquis and was a well-known and respected member of Parisian high society, yet by their standards they had come down in the world. Until I was made so welcome and made to feel at home by the whole family, I had certainly felt socially quite out of my depth.

'But it wasn't the story of Madame's illustrious forebears that kept us up until nearly midnight, but the remarkable story of Françoise, the eldest of Madame de Gaye's three daughters. By all accounts, she was something of a mischief maker as a child; a tomboy, always getting herself into trouble, or an "*enfant terrible*" as Madame de Gaye called her. There was some big family blow-up when she was studying medicine at the university in Paris, and she had walked out of the house, and taken up with some strange Bohemian artist in the Latin Quarter. He sponged off her for several years to subsidize his weird and wonderful lifestyle, and the group of anarchists who looked up to him as their Guru, at least when he was sober. Then she had a rather dramatic experience that completely changed her life. There was a terrible accident at the

Gare du Nord, several people were killed, and many others fatally injured. Françoise was called out to help, and she assisted one of the surgeons, who had to amputate both the legs of an eighty-year-old woman, who had been trapped underneath one of the carriages. It was Françoise's responsibility to look after her when she was moved into hospital, and it was this woman who changed her life.

'While attending her she noticed that she was wearing a miniature Franciscan cord beneath her clothes and when asked, she explained that she belonged to the Third Order of Saint Francis, but what impressed Françoise was the tremendous fortitude of the elderly woman, and the way in which she bore such terrible pain with such courage. There was something about her that she had never met in anyone else that made her feel drawn to her, not just to attend her as a doctor, but just to be with her. Then the poor old woman began to fail, and it was Françoise's job to tell her that there was nothing that could be done for her, and that she was dying. The moment she heard the words, she opened her arms and said, "Welcome, Sister Death," and from then on she refused any pain-killers of any sort, and even refused to eat unless she could be assured that the food had not been "doctored."

'Françoise said the pain must have been horrific and yet she never said a single word about the terrible suffering that she must have endured. Quite apart from anything else she was a medical phenomenon, and doctors and nurses from all over the hospital came to see how a patient could possibly bear such acute pain without seeming to feel anything at all. They all came to see a patient, but they left convinced that they had seen a saint. It wasn't just that she bore the pain with such fortitude, but it seemed to give her joy, and the profound peace that seemed to envelop her was communicated to all who came anywhere near her. There was something else a little more esoteric that would have seemed rather far-fetched had it not been experienced so regularly by someone like Françoise, who was a confirmed atheist at the time. There was a sweet pungent scent that seemed to envelop her, completely dispelling the stench of the gangrene that had set into her stumps. The strange thing was that some smelled it, and others didn't, although everybody without exception experienced the peace and joy that radiated from her until the end.

'Françoise was there when the end came, when she died literally in the "odor of sanctity." Just before she drew her last breath she pulled her hand out of the bed and pressed something into Françoise's hand and then died. When she opened her hand she found she was holding the Franciscan cord that the saintly woman had worn to the end. The message was clear, at least to Françoise.

'Within a week she had taken leave of her lover and his fellow anarchists, and had become reconciled to the Church that she had been brought up in, then she had sought out Père Claude, who promised to give her spiritual direction and finally to receive her into the Third Order of Saint Francis. Before he introduced her to the other secular Franciscans in Paris, he told her that she would have to spend a year as a novice, and this would mean submitting herself in obedience to the Novice Mistress. She readily agreed, quite unaware of the fact that the Novice Mistress was her own mother, whom she had not even seen for over three years.

'It was a happy reunion, and she obeyed her from the start, not only as a novice, but as a dutiful daughter, and she moved back into the old home at Cinq Rue de Magdebourg.

'After she had been received into the Third Order, she went to Africa, first to the Sudan, then to Uganda to work with other Franciscan Sisters and doctors in a large missionary hospital in the suburbs of Kampala. Alter about three years working in equatorial Africa she felt a pull towards a solitude that was denied her by the intensive work that she was engaged in as a missionary doctor. By chance she met a Franciscan Sister at a hospital at Shisong in the Cameroon, who told her of a unique community of Sisters, who lived high up in the Umbrian Hills above the Fonti del Clitunno, the source of the sacred river, the Clitumnus, where Roman soldiers bathed before battle a thousand years before Francis was born.

'When I asked Madame de Gaye about the Sisters, and to what Order they belonged, I was surprised to learn that they didn't belong to any Order at all. Technically they were not religious, at least in the legal or juridical sense. Their foundress, whom they preferred to call La Madre, had been a Franciscan Sister working in a busy hospital in Rome at the end of the First World War. When she became dissatisfied with her lot, because she could find little if any time for the prayer that meant so much to her, she took the matter to her superiors who weren't favorably disposed. By a rather clever piece of footwork, she managed to dodge the usual officials and bureaucrats who surrounded the Holy Father, and presented her case to him personally. He was so impressed with her, that he gave her permission to leave her Order while retaining her vow of chastity, to seek an environment for prayer for herself and for others of a like mind.

'After considerable heart-searching and journeying all over Italy, she met up with an Anglican in Florence, who had enough money to finance the venture at Campello sul Clitunno. Eventually others joined them and they moved to a remoter and more commodious hermitage a little further along the side of the hill, built around an ancient grotto or cave used by Saint Francis and other famous Franciscans as a place of prayer. They never felt the need or necessity to get ecclesiastical approval as a religious foundation, preferring a freedom and independence that has sustained them to this day. Their lifestyle is primarily eremitical and their inspiration is Franciscan. All the community belong to the Third Order of Saint Francis though this is never imposed on anyone seeking to join them.

'You could almost see the hermitage from Campello sul Clitunno, but you had to take a long circuitous route by way of the main road to get to the convent, and even then it was not easy. We had to leave the car at the end of a rough dirt track halfway up the hillside, and then walk for over a mile along a mule track to the hermitage that was perched high above the source of the sacred waters of the Clitumnus.

'Madame de Gaye explained that one of the Sisters would pick up the cases later with the convent mule, for we intended staying at the Eremo for at least three weeks. It's strange how you form a picture of someone you have heard a lot about only to have it smashed the moment you meet. I'm not quite sure what picture I had formed, maybe the pieces had not yet come together in my imagination, but at all events they were immediately banished into oblivion the very moment Françoise walked into the room. She was simply beautiful, not just with the made-to-measure beauty of the model that demands perfect symmetry of shape and form. She had all that, but she had much more. She was no mere mannequin, but a woman in full bloom, a bloom that was suffused as if by some inner light that radiated the warmth, the wit, and the well being of a mature and vital personality.

'Every feature of her face spoke, whether it was the way she tilted her head, arched her eyebrows, parted or pursed her lips, and they all spoke of a highly intelligent and articulate woman in her prime.

'"So this is how solitude sensitizes the soul," I thought, "to assimilate what it receives, and reflect outwards a new and unique embodiment of the One, who is the All in all."

'Whatever Françoise was supposed to have been before, she certainly was no more, that was for sure.

'The first thing I did when she came into the room was to blush as I had never blushed before, because I was so stunned by what I saw. The second thing was to thank God that the little stone parlor was so dark that my confusion could not be seen either by Françoise or by Madame de Gaye.

'My second reaction to Françoise was as unexpected as my first, for all that I had heard about her had not led me to believe that I would take such an immediate liking to her as a person. Rightly or wrongly I always tend to judge people by how they make me feel at home, how they enable me to be myself without feeling that I have to put on an act or make myself acceptable. Françoise made me feel completely at home. I felt I'd known her all my life. I never at any time felt obliged to do anything other than be myself, either then or at any other time in the future.

'We spent the first full day at the Eremo with Françoise. She showed us around and pointed out the paths that would enable us to explore the surrounding countryside for ourselves during the rest of our stay. After that first day we only met Françoise for one hour each evening after supper. Apart from that she continued to live the strict life of the hermit, to which she had given herself with total abandon. We, for our part, tried to do likewise; we had much to reflect upon and I had much to pray about. I couldn't have wished for a better environment for a retreat that was well overdue.

'At the beginning of the second week Madame de Gaye heard that Padre Guido, her one-time spiritual director, had just moved to Montefalco across the valley, and had taken up his appointment as guardian of San Fortunatus. She apologized for leaving us for a few days, but said she simply had to see the man who had helped her so much in the past, and whom she wished to consult about many matters concerning her future.

'I was pleased to have the opportunity of talking to Françoise on my own each evening, because I felt I could say things to her that I found difficult to speak about, even to her mother, and as I was soon to learn, she had things to say to me that left me in no doubt that she was already considerably advanced on the spiritual journey that I, too, wanted to embrace with something of the total commitment that had led her to Clitunno. I told her everything there was to know about myself, far more than I'd told anyone else. It was the first time I had spoken about such things to someone of my own generation. She showed an interest in details that I felt by instinct would be of no interest to the priests who had been of such help to me in the past, so that I hardly knew when to stop.

'Père Le Bec and the other priests who had been so helpful to me certainly listened and understood what I was saying to them, but Françoise listened with her heart.

'I suppose it's partly the difference between how a man listens and how a woman listens, but it was something more than that; something that neither of us quite realized at the time!

"'Well, I'm delighted you allowed Mother to organize you," she said. "She is a very good organizer, even though she organized you a bit too much in Florence, but I do understand what she was trying to do. The Renaissance was not all bad. Far from it. Where would medical science be today if it hadn't been for the rise of the natural sciences and the new scientific approaches that owe their origin to the great enlightenment?"

"'So you're taking your mother's side against me, are you?" I said, teasing.

"'Oh no, don't get me wrong, Peter. I know the point you're trying to make and I agree with you because I've experienced something of the worst excesses of what you call the activity-centered spiritualities. Don't forget I spent enough time on the Missions to know that the poor Africans have been evangelized by missionaries whose training and background have been dominated by a European presentation of Christianity that means little to them unless you can first Europeanize them to receive it.

"'You see, Peter, I experienced something of a second conversion when I went out to Africa. I thought I'd gone out to convert them with our particular brand of Christianity — only to find that it was they who converted me.

"'When I was running a clinic in the Sudan I was quite overcome by the practical Christianity that was the normal lifestyle of the people who were supposed to be 'pagans' — the people I had come to convert! I couldn't get over the way they loved one another, the way they shared everything they were given, not just with those in the same plight as themselves, but even with those who were better off. When I reflected on the so-called sophisticated Christian culture I had come from, I realized there was something radically wrong with our world, not theirs, something radically wrong with me, not them.

"'Strangely enough it was my experience of practical

Christianity lived out by so-called 'pagans' in Africa that has led me here to seek from God something of the goodness, the kindliness and the generosity of soul that I saw in them. Anyway, enough of my missionary experience, Peter. I can see I'm beginning to bore you."

"'Not at all, Françoise. What you say fascinates me for I was at one time seriously considering going to Africa myself as a missionary, but then I came to see that I'd better be converted myself before I had the cheek to start converting others. This is why I came to see how prayer was so important, but I'm afraid with all my big talk, and all the help I received I simply don't think I know the meaning of prayer any more, or to be more precise, I've come to a complete impasse.

"'The last few weeks in Franciscan Italy have been a great help to me, but the fact still remains that whenever I take the trouble to find what Père Claude calls consistent quality time for prayer, I simply get nowhere but more and more frustrated until I feel I'd be far better employed performing some useful service for my fellow man."

"'Believe me,' said Françoise, suddenly looking very serious. "There's nothing more important that you could be doing at this particular point in your spiritual journey than gently persevering in prayer."

"'But what am I to do?" I said.

"'You are to learn how to wait. That's what you must do. The highest teaching on prayer in the Gospel can be summed up in a single word, and that is waiting. It's all in the waiting. Now is the time when you must learn to wait.

"'Wisdom is finally found in waiting at the foot of the Cross, where all wisdom is to be found — the wisdom that is a stumbling block to the Jews and a folly to the Greeks."

"'But all this sounds a bit too much like quietism to me. I want to know what I can do."

'Françoise laughed. "Oh Peter, you do make me laugh. All your talk about the harm done by post-Renaissance spirituality.

All your talk about the activity-centered spiritualities and how they've forgotten the true meaning of prayer, and here you are wanting to join them, because you still want to be in control of your own spiritual destiny. Wherever you begin in prayer you will always come to the point when you find that you can't pray at all; that you can't do anything at all but wait upon God Who alone is in control. But this has to be learned as you wait, not just for months but for years at the foot of the Cross. This is where the mystical life really begins to unfold, and you want to cut and run before you've even started.

"'All the graces and helps you've received up to now have been given to support you at this moment. Now you must learn one of the hardest lessons of all. You must learn to wait upon God at the foot of the Cross. This is where all sinners are led to be made into saints, and we are all sinners. This is why the great Fathers of the Church saw Mary Magdalene as the perfect model for the Church. This is why she is depicted holding on, waiting at the foot of the Cross — to show all who would follow Christ that that's where all sinners are led to be sainted. Did you go to San Marco in Florence?"

"'Yes, I did."

"'Then you will have seen the paintings of Fra Angelico in room after room, depicting Saint Dominic at the foot of the Cross, waiting in prayer, just as Francis is painted in the same posture by other great mediaeval painters. They are all waiting for the Pleroma, for the outpouring of the Holy Spirit. No one knows when He will come. It may be in the third hour, the sixth or the ninth hour. Nobody knows when. All that is known is that He will come at an hour when we least expect Him like a thief in the night. Our job is to be ready and prepared with the wise virgins."

"'And how do we do that?" I said, thinking that at last there was something I could do.

'Again Françoise laughed. "Peter, you really are incorrigible. All right, I'll tell you what you can do while you wait. You can continue to practice the repentance of the heart as best you can, and that means as gently as you can, by using the means of prayer that help you most to keep turning and opening your heart, so that it is always ready and available to receive the One who will come when you least expect Him. If you are asleep when He comes, or if you run out of oil, if your heart's desire is no longer burning then you cannot welcome Him in.

"'Then there is something further that you can do. You can do the best you can to free your heart from the distractions and the temptations that prevent you from continually turning to God in prayer. If your heart is waiting on something else or someone else, then it can't be waiting on God, so you must try to seek out and extinguish at its source anything outside of prayer that fuels and fires the distractions inside of prayer. In other words, if you think you can put down the morning's crossword and have instant quality time for prayer, don't be surprised if you spend half your time trying to work out the name of a South American quadruped in four letters beginning with Z, and don't think you can switch off your favorite soap opera and switch straight on to God, because you'll spend most of your time trying to solve the marital problems of a. family that doesn't exist outside of the television studio. And so it's up to you to take a good hard look at the pleasures and pastimes that seduce you and the pet passions that draw your heart's desire away from God in prayer.

"'Now, Peter, don't misunderstand me. Remember what Père Claude said. I'm not saying give up television, crossword puzzles or novels or anything of that sort, but only give them up insofar as they prevent you from having consistent quality time for God each day. All this is part of the asceticism of the heart that you must practice, as you try to wait patiently, and attentively at the foot of the Cross.'

"'Yes, I do see what you mean," I said, and I did see what she meant quite clearly with my mind, but I was innocently unaware of the pent up passion that was going to plague me in the months ahead.

"'But that's not all," said Françoise. "You'll be delighted to know there is something further that you can do, for you must also try as best you can to continue the repentance that you have been practicing inside of prayer, outside of prayer, as you try to turn and open yourself to God in your neighbor in need. At the end of the day the quality of your loving inside of prayer will be judged by the quality of your loving outside of prayer. Nobody can see your love of God, but they can see your love of Man, and it will be by that love that they will judge the quality of your love of God. Saint John makes this quite clear.

"'Padre Angelo often comes over from Monte Casale to give us talks and hear our confessions. Last month he told us the story of two young novices who visited Saint Francis shortly before his death. The legend has it that they first asked the saint how he would know when he had arrived at true Christian prayer, and Francis answered without hesitation, 'By the love you have for your neighbor.' Then the second novice asked, 'And how can we tell when we have arrived at perfect Christian prayer?' Once again the answer came without hesitation, 'By the love you have for your enemies.' That quality of loving cannot be generated by Man's own endeavor, no matter how hard he tries. It is pure gift. That's why it will always be the authentic sign of genuine sanctity.

"'Tongues, prophecy, healing, miracles and wonders of every kind can be simulated, and even if they are genuine they are no sure sign of sanctity — but consistent selfless and unconditional love of others, to the point of love of enemies always is, whether the person is a professed Christian or a professed pagan.

"'As our spiritual life deepens through prayer, we allow God's love to come closer and closer to us, and as it does so it begins to highlight the imperfection and impurity of our love in comparison. This is the beginning of a mystical purification that must continue until every barrier to God's love has been removed from our hearts. Now in order to facilitate this inner purification we must accept the sinfulness that we see being laid bare, as the love of God comes closer and closer, and then we must express it in the Sacrament of reconciliation, so that we can be forgiven, and the source of the sinfulness within us can be purified away.

"'This is why confession was always seen as so important by the desert fathers.

"'When a monk went into the desert, he went in search of an abbot — a spiritual father who would guide him towards God. Now it was well known and understood that as the monk was directed towards God, and came to experience the power of the Holy Spirit in his life, then his own weakness and sinfulness would be progressively laid bare. As he saw his own sinfulness highlighted, then he would confess his sinfulness to his spiritual father. It was only later that the Church insisted that such a confession would only be considered sacramental if it was made to a priest, but this was not so in the early days when holiness was the only qualification that the monk sought in his spiritual guide.

"'I came across an old spiritual handbook, written for knights, in our library only a few days ago and it said that every knight should confess himself to a priest before a battle, and if he could not find a priest he should confess to his squire, and if he could not find his squire, he should confess to his horse! I don't think equine confession is sacramental, but it is no doubt salutary, at least from a psychological point of view, and I suppose that's the point of the story. But sacramental confession has a more profound and deeper significance, because the humility involved in submitting one's sinfulness to another in the Sacrament, acts as a magnifying glass as it were, that directs the purifying rays of God's love to the source of the sinfulness within. Then it can be burnt away, in what some Fathers of the Church have called the second baptism of fire.

"'I am sorry," said Françoise, "that was a bit of a mouthful. Let me explain the point I am trying to make. When my brother Bernard was a little boy, I bought him a magnifying glass for Christmas to help him identify the different stamps in his collection, but he soon found another use for my gift, as he found that he could use the glass to direct the rays of the sun upon little pieces of paper and set them alight. A good and sincere confession is an act of humility that acts as a magnifying glass that directs the fire of God's love to burn away all and everything in our hearts that prevents God's love from entering in.

"'So you see, Peter, have no fear. There's more than enough for you to do while you are waiting at the foot of the Cross, without feeling that you are falling into quietism. First you can practice repentance inside of prayer by using the means of prayer you find best for you, to keep gently trying to turn and open your heart to God. Second, you can continue the same process outside of prayer, as you learn the prayer without ceasing, by continually turning to God in your neighbor in need. Then third, you can so organize your daily lifestyle, that it becomes the perfect context for this prayer without ceasing, as you try to balance time for work, time for rest and time for prayer in a perfect harmony so that moderation always keeps pride within bounds.

"'Then finally, when you've done your best, and God begins to do His best, confess everything that surfaces under the influence of His love so that all can be purified away by the baptism of fire that first purifies you before setting you alight with the fire that you must communicate to others. All this is the asceticism of the heart that is at the core of any authentic spirituality, but never forget that from wherever you start you will always end up at the foot of the Cross, where you will have to learn to wait.'

"'I think that is what I find most difficult of all,' I said.

"'I know you do, Peter, because so do I. So do we all. Do you know why? Do you know why all of us hate waiting for anything? It might be waiting for a letter or for a phone call, or for a bus or a train, or an airplane, or whatever. We hate waiting because it means that we are not in control, and we love to be in control of our lives, and of other people's lives for that matter, if we are given the chance — that is the pride in us that is the root of all sin.

"'What I am saying is not personal to you, Peter. It is personal to everyone. When you are left to wait at the foot of the Cross, you'll learn patience, and you'll learn it the hard way, which is I'm afraid the only way that we will ever learn it, and that means by being patient, practicing patience, not just for days but for weeks and months, and even years.

"'It's here at the foot of the Cross that we finally learn in blood, sweat and tears that we are not in control, because the time comes when we can't do anything, not even pray, not even resist the temptations that seem to overwhelm us, never mind the distractions that assail us continually. There we have to experience for long periods of time our utter helplessness, when our whole life seems to be in ruins. This is the place where humility is finally and painfully learned; the humility that makes us realize that of ourselves we can do nothing. We thought we knew this truth at the outset of our spiritual journey — but we only knew it in our heads. Now it is learned in every fibre of our being, and it is this realization that is the final deathblow to the pride that has ruled us up to now, that finally opens us out more completely than ever before to Another Who, when He chooses, begins to make His home within us, to reign from where the 'Old Man' reigned before.'

"'Thank you so much, Françoise. You have summed up everything so simply.'

"'Not at all, don't thank me Peter, thank Père Claude. He would have said all these things to you anyway had he not been moved to Lyon.'

"'Yes, I know,' I said. 'He had already begun to talk about the asceticism of the heart shortly before he had to leave Paris. Tell me, what happens when God begins to work in a person who has learnt to wait in patience at the foot of the Cross? How does God begin to work in a person whose pride has been at least in some measure destroyed?'

"'Don't ask me, Peter. Please don't be deceived. I'm just a beginner, as you are. You have to ask someone holier than me.'

"'Can I write to you?' I said suddenly.

'"Yes, of course," said Françoise without hesitation. "We can support one another from afar through prayer. What are your plans, Peter, after your profession?"

'"Well, I'll spend some time with my parents in Manchester. Then I'll visit my brother at East Bergholt, and then I'm going to spend a month with a fellow student in the Outer Hebrides. He said that there is a chance that I could get a job the following year in the local school, so I intend looking around and perhaps making my home out there."

'"Be sure that I will always be with you in spirit, and you must keep in touch, and let me know how things work out."

'I think it was Shakespeare who said, parting is such sweet sorrow, and he was right. What sorrow it was to leave Clitunno. It was a sorrow for I had fallen in love with the place, and had been so happy there, getting to know Françoise and all the other Sisters who were so good to me, and whose simple transparent goodness was itself the only imprimatur that really mattered for the lifestyle they lived. But it was a sweet sorrow, too, for I'd found something, or rather someone, who so far had been missing from my life. I'd been blessed with two good brothers, but no sister. Now Françoise would be my sister, and I'd do my best to be a brother to her.

'I was so innocent, so guileless, that I jabbered all the way to Monte Casale with Madame de Gaye about her wonderful daughter, and the sister I had found in her. If I had seen and been able to interpret the looks that she was giving me, then I would at least have kept my mouth shut, but the truth is I really hadn't realized that something had just happened to me that had never happened before, but Madame de Gaye had!'

* * * * * * * * * *

I was dying to read the next typescript, but I simply had to get some work done if I was going to get through before I was due to leave. I wrote a sort of general letter that Father James picked up the following morning to be copied by the Sisters at the convent, and I put off reading the last typescript until I'd earned the right to read it, by addressing all the envelopes to Peter's correspondents, and by sorting out all his personal affairs. I still resorted to the well-proven, if rather infantile practice of promising myself little rewards that could not be enjoyed until all the work had been successfully completed. As you have no doubt already guessed, I'm afraid I'm still just an overgrown school-boy who's never really grown up, even though my thirtieth birthday has been dead and buried long since.

On the evening of the **7** third day Father James brought back two hundred duplicated copies of the letter I had composed and he brought with him exciting news. Peter's boat had been found, drifting almost two hundred miles north of the Shetlands. Interestingly enough, it had been spotted by the mine-sweeper H.M.S. Wasperon and, after examination, left at Mallaig so that it could be returned to its rightful owner, or at least his next of kin.

Father James explained to me that one of the fishing boats from Eriskay had towed it across the sea the night before. Three interesting things had emerged from an on the spot examination of the boat by Naval experts. One was that the immersion test was applied to the boat's timbers, and this enabled them to prove that the boat had been at sea continually since the morning of Peter's departure from Castlebay en route for Calvay.

The second was that the boat's rigging had been neatly tied up before the boat had been abandoned, and third, the tow rope had been cut cleanly with some sharp instrument, probably a knife, leaving twenty feet of rope dangling in the water.

"What did all this add up to?" I asked Father James.

"I just don't know," he said, "but one thing is for certain. Peter's boat was definitely towed by another boat of some description at some time or other, and another thing, the rigging on Peter's boat was folded neatly away by a hand other than Peter's. The skipper of the Thistle who towed the boat to Eriskay can vouch for this for he knows Peter well and knows how he ties up his rigging."

"Does all this mean that Peter is alive?" I said, quite unable to suppress my excitement.

"No, it doesn't," said Father James. "But," he said, pausing, pursing his lips and raising his eyebrows, "it does just mean there is hope where there was no hope before."

"Let's have a dram on it," he suddenly said, changing key and delivering one of his infectious smiles as he pulled a flask of Scotch out of his inside pocket.

After he left I got into bed and opened the last of Peter's typescripts. I had almost finished addressing the envelopes and I couldn't wait any longer to find out how he had fared at Monte Casale, and to see if he had any further contact with the young woman with whom he had obviously fallen in love.

FROM MONTE CASALE TO SAN GIOVANNI ROTONDO

'Imagine if you can an ancient and archetypal Franciscan hermitage, designed by Walt Disney, bent and buckled with age and reeking with atmosphere — then place it high up on a hillock, surrounded by thickly wooded slopes with magnificent views of the valley below, and there you have it — Monte Casale. A place of solitude and prayer since it was first given to Saint Francis, hardly half a dozen years after he was first called to contemplation.

'The day after I arrived Madame de Gaye left for Paris and Padre Angelo, the guardian, called me into his cell to welcome me personally to the sacred sanctuary, and invite me to full participation in the lifestyle lived by himself and his little community. He was a small fat jolly man, built for comfort not for speed — but he was always quick enough when anyone was in need of the care and compassion for which he was renowned. It was quite easy to see why he was the most popular Superior in the province.

'"Please don't be deceived by appearances," he said. "A

Franciscan friary is a place where sinners come together to support each other in a life of repentance. There is only one community of saints and that's the other side of the grave. I am called the guardian, not the Superior, because Saint Francis saw that Brother Jesus came not to lord it over anybody, but as a servant to serve the needs of others humbly — and so he insisted that in a Franciscan Brotherhood there should be no authority figure, but only a Brother raised up for a time to be at the service of the others. He felt that no one should ever be called an abbot, or a prior, or given any other title that would speak of superiority, but only of humble service. The titles warden, guardian, or minister, are the only ones ever given to a Brother, and they are only given to remind him of the role for which he has been raised up for a time. The greatest service that anyone can perform for others is to lead them to the fullness of love, which is the deepest desire of every human being.

'"The fullness of love is here, at the center of our penitential community, made present daily in the sacred mysteries, when God becomes present to us all in and through the glorified power of His Son Jesus. This sacred mystery is bursting with enough, and more than enough, creative life and energy to transform not just us, but the whole of humanity, beyond all our hopes and dreams. It sometimes frightens me to realize that the most effective way that I can lead them to this love is to go myself to be transformed, in such a way that my Brothers can see for themselves by the example of my life, what must be embodied in their lives. If I encourage in words alone, then my words will remain unheard for no one will listen to the words of a hypocrite.

'"The authority I have been given, like all authority in the Church from the highest to the lowest, is to help create an environment for those I am committed to serve, so that they can have the space and time in which to respond to the fullness of God's love. This means not just making sure that there is silence and solitude, without which such a response will soon become sterile, but to ensure that there is here a human and humane

119

environment in which each has time and space for his brother too, to give them a sympathetic ear, to support and encourage them, to respect their needs, understand their weaknesses, and make allowances for those not as fortunate as themselves. Then, a tolerant, accepting community can be built here by the Brothers, with a common aim to turn their lives unconditionally over to God.

"'It is my responsibility to try and achieve this, but unless each member of the community realizes that it is his responsibility also, then we will get nowhere. I am saying all this to you, because you will be one of us for the next four months or so, so I would like you to understand what our lifestyle is all about.'

"'Thank you, Padre Angelo,' I said. 'I'll do my best to fit in as well as I can, and please do tell me if I am rocking the boat in any way. I've never really had the purpose of Franciscan community life explained to me before. It makes sense. I can see now that with men of goodwill, it is possible to create such an accepting community.'

"'Oh dear,' said Father Angelo, "I can see I have not explained myself properly. The purpose of the Franciscan lifestyle is not to produce an accepting community, but a community of Brothers refashioned by the Holy Spirit into a Christian community, similar to the community of Christ and His disciples. The first apostolate then for Franciscans is to minister the love that they have received, to one another, so that the very community of God's life, the life of the Three in One, can be made flesh and blood in a human brotherhood that reflects the divine.

"'The Gospel does not say that you should just tolerate one another, make allowances for one another, build an accepting community with one another; it says you should love one another with the same love that Christ has for us. It then goes on to say that you should forgive one another seventy times seven, love not just your friends but your enemies too, and even pray for those who would torture you and put you to death. This is impossible for Man, as the Gospel itself states quite clearly.

"'Man's endeavor may well be able to generate, at least in

part, an 'accepting community,' but only God's endeavor can create a loving, caring, compassionate Christian community, that reflects the inner life of God here on earth."

"'Thank you, Padre," I said. "That makes many things clearer to me. You see I've been so busy criticizing the spirituality that I was brought up on that over-emphasized human endeavor, that I was in danger of going to the other extreme. I see now that although no human endeavor can create a Christian community, neither can God bring such a community to birth unless Man takes all the steps necessary to allow Him in."

"'Right," said Father Angelo, "but where many people are going wrong today is that because religious life is in need of renewal, they are turning all too readily to the rising socio-psychological sciences. They restate the Gospel in the language of sociology and psychology, and so they talk in terms of self-realization, becoming fully human, fully mature, building an accepting community, and so on, so that without realizing it they subtly lower the standards of the Gospel. They lower them to a level that makes them believe they are within Man's grasp with the methods and techniques culled, often uncritically, from an otherwise reputable branch of science, that is only in its infancy.

"'I think it is important to state the Gospel quite unequivocally and without watering it down in such a way that people cannot be deceived into believing that they can achieve it by their own endeavor. The Gospel says, 'Be perfect as God is perfect, be compassionate as God is compassionate, love one another as Christ loves you.' It does not talk of building an accepting community, but of a community in which the Father, the Son and the Holy Spirit are embodied in the very bodies of those who make up that community.

"'If anyone thinks that they are capable of making such a community by their own endeavor, and generating such love by their own ingenuity, then they are making a big mistake. The Gospel says again and again, I know you can't but I can if you only allow Me in. It is a Gospel that can only be heard by those humble enough to know their need of God, and so are prepared to turn to Him in their need. Here at Monte Casale we have much to do to try and create a human and a humane accepting community, but only as the best possible way in which to support one another in a life of continual repentance. This is the only way we can open our hearts to the only One Who can make us into a Christian community here on earth that is a sign of the brotherhood that is for all in heaven.

"'So you can see, Peter, human endeavor is essential in creating the environment Man needs to be fully open to God.

"'We must do our part so that God can do His part. Our part is to try continually to generate the human moral virtues necessary, such as tolerance, forbearance, respect for others and for the lifestyle to which we have committed ourselves, and so on, so that we can live together in the same friary supporting one another in responding to God. If genuine psychological insights and sociological expertise can help to do this, well and good, but they will never — I repeat never — be able to create a Christian community, and those who believe they can, are blind leaders of the blind.

"'The law has its part to play also. Now the law will never create community, but it can and must safeguard the right of individuals who want to respond to the only One who can. The law can and must, for instance, insist on times and places for silence and solitude, for no prayer life will ever grow without such an environment. Now when we have done all we can do to create the best possible environment for a communal response to God through repentance, then God can do His part. His part is to fill us with His own Spirit which will alone make us one as He is One, so that we can literally embody the prayer Jesus made for us all at the Last Supper."

'I spent the afternoon mulling over all that Padre Angelo had said, and I have often reflected on the important distinction that I first heard from him, because I think it needs to be made with greater urgency today than ever before. It's not that the insights of contemporary psychology have nothing to offer. They have much to offer, particularly if they offer to people the means of building a more human community together by making them more aware of their mutual needs and helping to heal the scars that prevent them becoming a full member of that community. But when all has been done, the real work begins, when men and women of goodwill radically support one another to receive the goodwill of God.

'In the evening of that day I began to work out my own timetable for the months ahead, based on what Padre Angelo had said, and the moderation that Père Claude had insisted upon. I couldn't believe my luck. Here I was in this beautiful and remote place of solitude with over four months before me to become ever more fully immersed in God, to recapture the brief moments of contemplation that I had experienced in Notre Dame, so that such prayer might become my daily spiritual diet and lead me on to the sanctity that I so deeply desired.

'How naive I was when I look back at myself at the beginning of those four months, expecting it would be my heaven on earth, when in fact it turned out to be my hell.

'Padre Angelo suggested Padre Fabiano as my spiritual director, to whom I would go for confession and instruction every Friday. He was a good solid religious, but a little too busy to spare too much time with a beginner like myself, especially as he had a deadline for the book he was working on. Once he had heard my confession, he would say a few well-chosen words lasting no more than three minutes, then give me absolution and turn back to his desk, so that I never had the opportunity to ask him for help or advice, even if I had wanted to do so. He was working on ancient monastic texts recently discovered in Ethiopia which has a monastic tradition as old, if not older, than the Egyptian monasticism about which I had often read.

'I had to report to another priest each morning, Padre Bernadino, who arranged the manual work that was part of my daily routine.

'He was a young man in his late twenties who looked exactly like the proverbial tall, dark and handsome stranger, who'd just walked out of a women's magazine. He had all the Latin looks and the Mediterranean manners that had already got him into more than enough trouble, as I found out later. The main ongoing job, to which I returned whenever more pressing work allowed, was the pruning of the vines in the small vineyard attached to the hermitage. Padre Bernadino seemed to be the only member of the community who resented my presence, or so I thought to begin with. He always seemed to be in a mood, a bad mood mostly, that would make him surly, sulky and generally difficult to relate to. I got the distinct impression that he was not living the eremitical life by choice, and that his presence at Monte Casale was not the result of his own personal preference. When he did deign to talk to me, it was usually about Rome where apparently he had been in his element, working with youth and dedicating his spare time to supporting the needy. Apparently Roma, who were at the bottom of the football league, fell into this category, until with his selfless devotion and tireless support they were able to return to their rightful place at the top.

'I also began to support Roma, and even prayed for their weekly success, so that at least the outset of the ensuing week would be a little more liveable than when they lost. I gathered that Dino, as he wanted to be called, had come to Monte Casale only three months before I arrived, and he came under some sort of unspecified cloud. Rumor had it that his youth club became all too successful when his brother, an agent in the world of show biz, arranged for international artistes to patronize it, mainly jazz artistes, so that his club became a mecca for trad jazz, not just in Rome but in the whole of Italy.

'Padre Dino was well known all over Rome as a clerical whiz-kid, a "*bon viveur*," and his name would always appear at the top of the list for all the trendy society parties. Whether they were true or not, nobody seemed to know, but suspicious rumors began to circulate about his relationships with attractive young actresses and other famous female personalities from the world of show biz. It was his superiors, not Padre Dino, who thought that the seclusion of Monte Casale would be just the place for him to pause for a time, to try to see the way his life was going, to see things in a clearer perspective.

'No doubt his superiors acted with the best of intentions but Dino didn't see it that way, nor did he see Padre Angelo as anything other than a jailor, and Monte Casale as a prison from which he would escape the moment the jailor was out of the house. He used to change into a grotesque Teddy-boy outfit halfway down the hill, and bundle his habit into an old suitcase that he would retrieve on his way back.

'On one occasion he was in such good spirits when he returned from one of his outings in Perugia that he didn't bother to change before arriving back at the friary, where he danced a "boogie woogie" to the amusement of the farm animals and half the community who witnessed the squalid little scene from a safe distance. However, Padre Dino did me no harm and, in fact, he came to like me. As time went by he began to lecture me on schools of theological thought that seemed best disposed to the lifestyle that he aspired to, and which he thought were far more human, and therefore far closer to the Gospels than the mediaeval make-believe world that his fellow friars had chosen to live in.

'My personal troubles really began when I started to pray in earnest once more, especially in the evening, after Compline when I had set aside a full three hours for the contemplative prayer that I felt sure would soon raise me to the heights of mystical union.

'At first I didn't realize what was going on. I just began to muse on the sister I had found, and on the mutual support that we would be able to give one another in the years that lay ahead. Then in the days ahead the endless delight I took in contemplating not God, but the sister I had supposed He'd given me, began to arouse deep and vital feelings within, that I felt sure no sister had aroused before though I'd never had one to judge. Perhaps things wouldn't have been so bad if I'd had more to occupy my mind, but the very solitude I had chosen made it quite impossible for me to avoid the desires and the longings that began to ravage every moment of the time I had set aside for God.

'I started to re-live the first moment when we had met, the conversation we had shared. Then it was the way she walked, the very movement of her body began to move me with feelings I'd never felt before, and then there was her voice; that irresistible French accent that I had found so attractive at the time began to send me into paroxysms of desire. I could hear that voice so clearly in my mind, as she left me at the end of our evening talks:

'"Bonsoir, Pierre, et dormez bien." The way she pronounced those 'R's' with that engaging Parisian accent was too much for me, and several times I found myself in tears in the contemplation of something, no someone, who was so dear to me and yet so unobtainable. I knew she would always be my sister and I would always be her brother, but I wanted so much more, and I knew she would recoil from me if she knew the half of it. She was so innocent, so pure, so utterly beyond me in every way that I began to wonder if she'd ever have looked at me twice had I not arrived with her mother.

'But then I was jolted back into a little more reality when I recalled her past. No, perhaps she wasn't the spotless virgin I wanted to make of her, but it wasn't she who was at fault. How could she be? It was that lousy lay-about who had seduced her that was to blame. At one moment I began to vent my anger against him in my mind; at another moment I was consumed with jealousy, because he had had, for some of the time, the woman I wanted for all time.

'My passions made a mockery of my prayer. I had no sooner stopped drooling over the past than I started planning for the future, writing and re-writing the letters in my mind that I began to send to her every other day; planning how I could see her again before I returned to Paris and then working out what I would say to her when we finally met. The morning Mass and the meditation that preceded breakfast seemed to last for ever, as I counted the minutes to the moment when the mail was due, willing the letter I tried to anticipate in my mind, wondering how she would answer the many innuendoes that I had used to try and induce her to reveal if there was even a flicker in her to match the flame that was in me.

'Then there would be that terrible anti-climax if no letter arrived, or if its contents failed to assuage the desire in me that weighed every word she used to interpret to my own advantage. No depression, however dark, that had descended upon poor Dino was darker than the depression that descended upon me when the postman's patronage passed me by. Life wasn't worth living, not for me, or for anyone who came into contact with me. On mornings like that, which were not infrequent, I would leave the vines to prune themselves, and vent my rage with the heavy-headed axe in the wood-shed.

'The prayer that I thought would have been my daily heaven became my daily hell. If the postman had not passed me by that day, and if the letter was to my liking, at least I could revel in pleasant thoughts, although I was always haunted by the realization that the fantasies that I conjured in my mind would never be realized in my life. But when the postman had passed me by, or if the letter he brought was not to my liking, I would suffer terrible depressions, punctuated by fits of anger, anger against myself, anger against everybody around me, anger against the so-called God of Love, who had given me a love for someone He had spoken for Himself — if that's fair, if that's God's justice, then I wanted none of it, and none of Him for that matter, if that's the way He treats a person who wants what is right and gives his life for it.

'All feelings for God finally evaporated, so I began to ask myself, "Where had He gone?" for He seemed to have disappeared from my life, and from the prayer that had once meant so much to me. Then I began to say, "Is there a God, or is He just a creature created by my own mind to cater to the deep desires and needs of my own impoverished personality?" All these temptations began to affect me outside as well as inside of prayer, so that I became a burden, not just to myself, but to the community who had so generously welcomed me into their midst.

'When Padre Angelo went to Clitunno just before Christmas, he took me with him, and I spent a whole ecstatic hour with Françoise that kept me going for weeks though I at no time gave any impression that I was more than a good friend or that she was more than a sister to me, or so I thought. All my troubles were compounded when Padre Dino began to outline his latest theory of the animus and the anima, which he had adapted from the Jungian psychology that he was always talking about. He argued that it was not Man but Mankind who were created in the image and likeness of God — and that means man and woman who reflected here on earth something of the inner nature of God. In God, the male and the female, the animus and the anima, are perfectly balanced in the One who is perfection itself. No man, therefore, he argued, can come to know God experientially except through a deep personal relationship with a woman, and vice versa. Only together can God's own image be reflected with any degree of perfection here on earth.

'It was an interesting theory, and he claimed it was backed up not just by Jung, but by many of the great Fathers of the Church.

'"But what about Jesus Himself?" I argued, "And the clear call to the celibate life that you find in the Gospels?"

'"That does not destroy my thesis," he said. "It reinforces it. Jesus's attitude to women was revolutionary, even the most conservative scholar would accept that, and the relationship He had with women was deep and personal, and part and parcel of His own personal growth into human maturity. Look at the love He had for Martha and Mary, or Mary Magdalene and the Samaritan woman, and other women too, who followed Him to the end. It was a celibate love but love none the less, a love for the opposite sex which complemented His maleness.

'"Read the lives of the saints — or some of our own Franciscan saints, for instance, and you will find that many of them had a relationship with a woman who loved, helped, and complemented them. Francis and Clare is the obvious example. There have been many Franciscan tertiaries who lived together as brother and sister in a celibate love that transcended the sexual, and enabled them to mirror the life of God on earth far more perfectly than any single-sexed Order has ever done."

'Well, you can imagine what all this did to me. I spent hours in the library going through the Fathers of the Church, reading Jungian psychology and some scriptural exegesis of Genesis to make more thoroughly my own, the ideas that I had all too readily and uncritically accepted from Dino. I hardly need to say why or detail the way in which my mind was working. If Dino was right, and I couldn't see how he was wrong, I could continue my vocation, not in a lesser but in an even fuller way by bearing witness to the fullness of God by continuing my journey with another whose femininity would complement my masculinity and vice versa. This would not necessarily be in a sexual way, but through a celibate love that would be an even more perfect sign of the fullness of love in heaven, when there would be no more marriage or giving in marriage.

'I was furious that Padre Angelo's next visit to Clitunno was immediately followed by a meeting in Rome, which prevented me from going with him to present my case to my very dear Françoise. By the end of February I could wait no longer. I simply had to see Françoise and talk to her about the future. I told Padre Angelo that I would be going to Montefalco for a few days to see the Padre Guardiano at San Fortunatus about my future plans. I explained that he was Madame de Gaye's spiritual director, and I had promised to visit him anyway before I left Italy.

'I won't bore you with the details of the travel arrangements that I had to make to get from Montefalco to Clitunno, because it is quite a saga in itself. The distance wasn't far as the crow flies, but it was a very long way by bus, taxi and Shanks's pony, but it was worth it. Anything would have been worth it to see dear Françoise again, even for a single moment.

'On my first two visits I was so overcome by her, and the love that I felt for her that I didn't talk about anything of any consequence, but on my third and final visit things came to a head when I began to open my heart to her. I told her that although the community at Monte Casale were kindness itself, I had been going through a daily hell in the place that I thought would have been my heaven. I told her that my prayer had not only completely disappeared, but that I had been plagued with terrible temptations that had been torturing me for weeks on end.

'I couldn't help feeling that Françoise became a little more distant the more personal I became in expressing my deepest feelings, as if she guessed where it was all leading; and so by some sixth sense I stopped short of the real temptation that I wanted to talk to her about. Instead I emphasized that the inner tensions that I was experiencing were even affecting my sleep. Some nights I hadn't slept at all. On other nights I was lucky if I slept for more than two hours.

'"Peter," she said, looking both concerned and clinical at one and the same time, "you must do two things. First, get more exercise, outside in the fresh air. Second, talk over the inner tensions and temptations that have been rising up within you with Father Angelo, or with one of the other priests."

'That did it. I jumped to my feet in a fury.

'"Oh, thank you. Thank you so much, doctor, for the consultation. So sorry to have taken up so much of your time." And with that, I went out slamming the parlor door behind me as loudly as I could. But I had gone no more than a few paces down the passage-way outside when I turned round and went back into the room.

'"Oh, Françoise, I'm sorry, I'm sorry, I'm sorry," I said. "But don't you see that I love you. It's my love for you that has been possessing me in prayer and out of prayer, and every moment of my day. I can't help myself. Is it all wrong? Isn't love God's greatest gift? Isn't it He who has given me this gift, and has given me that gift for you? I'm sure of that now. I have discussed these matters with one of the priests at Monte Casale, and he believes that the love of man for woman can be the most potent and powerful witness on earth to the community of life in God in heaven."

'I went on talking rapidly, explaining Dino's theory and supplementing it with what I had read for myself, and exemplifying my case with Franciscan tertiaries, who had lived together as brother and sister, and helped each other to the heights of sanctity.

'Françoise's attitude to me had changed when I came back into the room in tears to declare my love for her. She had softened, but the more I outlined my theory, she became more and more distant again.

'Finally she said, "Peter, the priest you've been speaking to is Padre Bernadino, isn't it?"

'"Well, yes," I said. "How do you know him?"

'"How do I know him?" she exclaimed. "I think almost the whole of Italy knows him, and the scandals that surrounded him, and the trendy set that he mixed with in Rome — it was all over the newspapers at the time.

'"He has already had two canonical warnings; one more and he will be out, and if I had spoken up he would be out by now."

'"How do you mean?"

'"He came here to give us a talk when Padre Angelo was ill last September. I didn't know about him at the time, and so I was taken in by him. His talk was full of all the things that you have been saying to me and I was quite impressed because theoretically his ideas have some merit. Later he managed to get me alone in the parlor and began to talk to me about celibate love, and how man can reach out and touch the feminine in God, through His image made flesh in woman. Then he began to reach out to touch the feminine in me in a way that enabled me to see him for what he was — if Mother Superior had not walked in by pure accident, I hate to think what he would have done. It was she who told me all about him later, and I am telling you about him now so you won't be deceived by him or he will lead you astray, for he has a good mind and knows just how to mix good sound theology with dross, to intellectualize his own disreputable lifestyle, and legitimize the illegitimate desires that will lead him to ruin.

"'It is only the generosity of his superiors that have given him what is now his last chance.'"

'I was so flabbergasted by all this, so completely deflated by what I'd heard that I was unable to outline the plans I had made in my mind to set before Françoise, for a future that I hoped we would be able to share together as Franciscan tertiaries.

'We parted on good terms, but not on the terms that I had hoped for when I had made my way along that long mule track for my last interview with the woman I loved.

'I received a letter from Françoise four days after I returned to Monte Casale that shattered me. It was kindly, no doubt about it. It was sisterly, too, no doubt about that either, but it was final. She told me plainly that she had taken a private vow of chastity, and she had taken it for life. Only Rome could dispense her from it, and she had no intention of petitioning for such a dispensation. She said she loved me as a sister and always would, but my feeling for her made it quite clear that we could no longer meet in the way we had met in the past.

'She said she would no longer write to me, and my letters would be returned unopened. She apologized if the tone of her letter sounded harsh, because she still had, and would always have a sisterly affection for me that would keep me in her prayer for always. She wished me well for my profession and said she would get news of me from her mother, and if nothing gave her reason to believe it was the wrong thing to do, she would write to me on the tenth anniversary of my profession, when time may well have tempered the mutual feelings that made it imperative for us both to pursue our different vocations without any further personal relationship.

'I felt numb and broken when I had finished the letter. I got the day off, and found a lonely spot high up in the forest, behind the hermitage where I burst into uncontrollable tears of grief, and I sat with my head in my hands for hours with nothing and no one to console the desperation that I felt within me. I had never thought I could be so deeply hurt, so utterly broken, as I was that day.

'I nearly jumped straight out of my skin when I felt a gentle hand placed on my shoulder. I turned round to see the kindly face of a friar whom I'd seen only rarely in the hermitage. Sometimes I had seen him at Mass; sometimes I had seen him at the back of the chapel, late in the evening, lost in prayer, but I had never seen him in the refectory or in the recreation room. I had been so preoccupied with myself these last months that I never got round to asking anyone who he was. He was of more than average height, but he had stooped gracefully into middle age, and so looked somewhat smaller than the man he was. He had clean-cut classical features that looked as if they'd originally been set in bronze, and then made molten again to be re-set in a softness and sympathy that had been forged in suffering.

"'Forgive me, Padre," I said, "but I feel so terrible, I feel as if my heart is going to break and I just do not know what to do."

"'It's not Padre," he said kindly. "Just call me Antonio. I'm not a member of the community though Padre Angelo is very kind to me, and allows me to make full use of the hermitage whenever I like. I live on my own, a little further up the hillside."

"'You mean you are a hermit?" I said.

"'Yes, I suppose you could call me a hermit," he said. "I belong to the Third Order of Saint Francis and I've been living there for over ten years now. But that's enough of me. What's the matter? Please feel free to talk to me, but first, come back to my little home, it's too cold out here to talk for long."

'He lived in an over-sized hut made of stone that he'd furnished for himself, and made very cosy in an austere sort of way.

'When I'd sat down he said, this time in impeccable English, "Now tell me everything in your own language, I know you are a linguist, but Italian is not your strongest point, is it?"

"'No," I admitted. "But your accent tells me that English is yours."

"'Well, I have spent some time in England," he said. "But that's a long story, my story. What's important now is your story, please tell me everything. I'll not betray your confidence to anybody."

'I told him everything, and what a relief it was to get it all off my chest, even if he could not understand the pain of love found, and love lost, that was tearing me apart.

"'My dear friend, I do understand. Believe me, I do understand. Listen to me now and to my story for it may help you. It is a story that only Padre Angelo has heard, and that ten years ago. I have not always been a hermit. I was once a young student like yourself, studying physics at Milan. God had given me everything, a good home, good and loving parents, a good brain too, that promised a brilliant academic career. When I graduated, I went to Rome and got my Ph.D. And then I was offered the chair of physics, much to the consternation of the other applicants, most of whom were twice my age.

"'In the second year of my appointment, I fell in love with one of my students, a woman of extraordinary beauty. She was an aristocrat from Florence, a direct descendant of the Medicis and proud with it, until she fell in love with me, and trampled on her pride to favor the son of a Milanese baker. Her family would not hear of the marriage, so we eloped and boarded a ship bound for England. We were married aboard that ship by the Captain, but we were married again in church the moment we arrived in London. Oh, we were deliriously happy, and I managed to get a lectureship at Cambridge where we lived for three years; my happiness was complete when my dear, darling wife became pregnant. Then eight months later she died in childbirth. Oh, I cannot tell you what I went through, what I suffered. I was a broken man in a foreign country, and an unwelcome foreigner too, because war had broken out and Mussolini had allied himself with Hitler. I only managed to get out of England by the skin of my teeth, otherwise I could have been interned for the duration of the war.

"'When I got back to Rome, I had something of a breakdown and became something of a bum, sleeping rough and begging for pennies to keep my body and soul together, although I often wondered why I bothered. I gave up God and His religion. How could there be a God — a loving God who would not do to the meanest dog what He had done to me? I went from bad to worse. I'd always had a good hand for art, so I bought myself some chalk and began drawing pictures on the pavement. At least it was better than begging. Most of what I made went into drink, that had already made an alcoholic of me.

"'Times were hard and the price of drink got higher and higher. It was then that I heard of Padre Pio and of San Giovanni Rotondo, so I gathered what few belongings I had and I made for the South.'"

"'What was it that led to this conversion?'" I said.

"'This wasn't a conversion,'" he said, "I went to San Giovanni Rotondo not for conversion but for money. Where the pilgrims are, there the pennies will be, or so I thought. I began to draw saints, and I did quite well until someone suggested drawing the good Padre whom everyone had come to see. So I did, but nobody was satisfied with my work. After all, I was only copying the pictures I had seen in the shops, so I decided to go and see the man himself.

"'It was the first time I had been to Mass since my wife died, and it had a dramatic effect upon me, not the Mass itself I have to admit, but the man at the altar, the man I came to make my model. Oh yes, he was to become my model, but in an entirely different way than I had expected when I entered that church. It was when he turned round to give his final blessing that his eyes met mine and I knew it was no accident — something happened then, deep down within me. I'll never be able to explain. It took me four days to screw up the courage, but finally I went to confession.

"'When I went in he just turned to me and said, 'Antonio, my son, God has forgiven you, has forgiven you everything.' Tears were streaming down my cheeks, then he simply said, 'Go, and change your life.' I've never been the same since. Later he arranged with Padre Angelo for me to come to Monte Casale, and to stay with the community for a time. After nine months I left them and came up here, but I keep in touch with Padre Pio, he has accepted me as one of his spiritual sons, and I return to see him every second year."

'At the beginning of that day I wouldn't have believed I would ever smile again, but the transparent goodness of Antonio, and the story he told me left me in no doubt of his compassion and understanding, that touched something deep down within me.

'"It's providential that I met you, Antonio, because you're the only one who can help me," I said.

'"I'll do all I can," he said.

'"I had thought that one day I would become a hermit like you," I said, "But now I think I'll have to think again. I don't think I'm cut out for the solitary life."

'"Why not?" said Antonio.

'"Well, who's ever heard of a hermit who can't pray? I once thought I could but now I know I can't"

'"Oh no, that's not true," said Antonio. "Your problem is not that you can't pray, it's that you don't know what prayer is. You may think that these last months when you've been battling against terrible distractions have been a waste of time, because they prevented you from what you thought prayer was all about, but they have not been a waste of time at all. Prayer does not grow because temptations gradually disappear; it grows because they get stronger and stronger and the ensuing battle is the place where true Christian prayer reaches its height if people only knew it.

'"Beginners always think it's about having nice feelings and emotional highs. Romantics think it's all about having feelings of inner peace, and the latest Gurus — who are beginning to come back from the East — seem to think it's all about having high states of transcendental awareness and mastering the techniques that lead to Nirvana. As you must know, when Francis came back from his first serious attempts at prayer, he came back so exhausted from his conflict with the temptations that rose from the 'Old Man' within, that even his friends didn't recognize him. The struggles of the inner man had marked the outer man with a depression that could even be seen in his physical appearance.

"'Remember Jesus in His prayer, in His conflict with the power of Evil in the desert and later in Gethsemane, and you won't forget that authentic Christian prayer beyond the first beginnings is the place where hell is kicked out of you by the power of heaven, that you endeavor to allow in by your inner repentance of heart.

"'To begin with, God often gives you an experience of His presence that leaves you in no doubt Who is at work. Initially this is usually of short duration and is but a glimpse of what will be of longer duration, when the purification about to begin is brought to completion.

"'This is what happened to you in Notre Dame. It was strength for the conflict that you have already begun. But believe me, Peter, the spiritual conflict is a fifteen-rounder and you're hardly halfway through the first. When the asceticism of the heart opens your heart to wait upon God, it does not mean that your heart has been changed; the change hasn't yet begun. It just means that it's ready and available to God for the change that only He can bring about.

"'Man has to make his heart available for God to act, but only God can change it. The pain that all must experience who want to travel on beyond first beginnings is the pain caused by the irresistible force of God's love as it strikes the immovable object, which is man's obstinate heart. Forgive me if I revert to my own subject to make my point. Do you remember the question that was asked in physics class when you were at school? What happens when an irresistible force strikes an immovable object?"

"'Yes,' I said. 'I do. Heat is generated.'

"'Precisely. The same principle in the physical order applies to the spiritual order. When the irresistible power of God's love strikes the immovable object of a proud, intractable human heart, then heat is generated. It is the heat that comes from the fire of the Holy Spirit, and it begins here on earth. It is the purgatorial purification that all must go through before entering into union with God, on the simple principle that unlike things cannot be united. Somewhere between now and union with God a likeness has to be created within us. The Holy Spirit has been sent to create that likeness by purifying us of all, and everything, that prevents us from being united with God.

'"The saint is a person who has already passed through their purification here on earth, and so can become a most perfect instrument that God is able to use, to communicate to others in need the love they have received. Don't believe the pseudo-mystics from the East or the West who try to deceive far too many people today into believing that true mysticism is primarily about high states of consciousness, or esoteric experiences with accompanying phenomena of dubious authenticity. They attract the spiritual butterflies who are always looking for new seductions on which to settle, at least for a while.

'"If you are ever in doubt, turn to the Gospels and see Jesus at prayer; see Him at war with the power of Evil throughout His life in Palestine until His death in Jerusalem. True Christian prayer always involves a fight, a battle, a conflict, that is fiercest in the desert where no escapism can lure the believer from the repentance that exercises the muscles of the heart like nothing else on earth.

'"When I was lecturing in Cambridge, the students of Peterhouse, where I resided, were invited to enter a tug-o'-war team in a local competition as part of the celebrations for the Coronation. When they saw the other teams from the local villages in action, they were ready to throw in the towel before they had even started. Then one of the dons, who once played rugby for Wales, said they'd beat all comers if they were prepared to train. For five months they trained on the football field every afternoon without fail, until their muscles had grown and become hardened to the task ahead of them. To cut a long story short, they won the competition outright and pulled their opponents into the River Cam, over which the final competition took place. They were the toast of the town for beating some of the heftiest farmers I have ever seen. They did it by persistent and consistent practice that enabled the muscles of their bodies to generate the power and strength that made them unbeatable even by the strongest opposition.

"'The self-same process takes place in prayer. If you are prepared to give consistent daily time for practicing the asceticism of the heart through repentance, then gradually the most important muscles that a person possesses are developed. They are the spiritual muscles of the heart that open that heart ever more fully to God. As this happens they allow an other-worldly power and strength in, that makes the weakest the strongest, for whom even the impossible becomes possible. The reason why so few people journey on beyond their first fervor in prayer is that the exercise becomes so hard and taxing, and the temptations become so hard to bear, that they prefer to seek the solace of a job well done, or a pleasure enjoyed, to the tortuous and testing struggle of prayer beyond first beginnings.

"'The prayer that exercises the muscles of the heart through an endless spiritual tug-o'-war against distractions and temptations is exhausting in the extreme, precisely because a person is exercising the muscles of the highest faculty that they possess.

"'The young men who won the tug-o'-war tournament across the River Cam were not surprised when their exertions left them exhausted, nor is the footballer, the tennis player or the swimmer at the end of their exertions. Only half an hour in the pool is enough for most of us, but we are surprised when we are tired at the end of half an hour of spiritual tug-o'-war in prayer, when we have been exercising the most important, and the most under-used muscles we possess.

"'Let me exemplify my point by referring you to the first principle of thermodynamics. *Therm* comes from a Greek word meaning *heat*, and *dynamics* also comes from a Greek word meaning *work*. The first principle of thermodynamics is this: work is heat, and heat is work, and the work that is generated in the prayer I am trying to explain produces the highest form of energy, which is love, when the believer turns from temptation at its highest to love at its fullest. This is why the certain sign of a would-be saint that baffles those who stand on the side-lines, is the continual exhaustion from the inner conflict.

"'Nobody, not even the doctors, can make head nor tail of the strange draining illnesses, about which everyone has their own theory, but nobody in fact knows, because the real meaning of prayer and the spiritual journey is sadly known to so few today. During the last few months you have been exercising the muscles of your heart more regularly, and with greater energy than ever before. You've been traveling fast, though you may not think you've been traveling at all. As you have been trying to turn back to God, sometimes in pitch beyond pitch of grief, then you've been more open to God than at any other time in your life, and so the love of God has been working within you in a way that will gradually transform you into the Man you have freely chosen to follow.

"'Now, let us see how this process of transformation is brought about. Please do excuse me for once more resorting to the only branch of knowledge that I really know anything about. It was your own Sir Isaac Newton who discovered a truth that will enable me to describe how God's love first penetrates a human being before being channeled into human acting so that a disciple becomes an apostle, propelled from within by the power of the God Who possesses him.

"'Newton discovered that although light is colorless, it contains within itself all the colors of the spectrum. They remain unseen until they strike a prism that reflects and refracts them in such a way that all the colors of the rainbow are clearly visible for all to see. Now, it's exactly the same with the love of God, which is always available to all who would open their hearts to receive it. When that love is allowed to shaft down into the human heart, it first purifies it, and then it refines it into a prism that refracts and reflects God's love into every part of the human personality, until it becomes visible to onlookers by the way it manifests itself in human behavior.

"'The Christ-like care and compassion, the super-human

quality of selflessness and sacrifice, and the heroic virtues that are generated by the Spirit-filled apostle, are but the outward expression of the divine life already possessing them from within. The exercise of the human heart in prayer then allows the divine life in, so that it is transposed through human *being* into human *acting*. Not only does this love further strengthen the muscles of the heart, but it opens that heart out from the inside to receive even more of the love that it has already received.

"'Now the true Christians are fashioned so they are able to return the love received in kind to the One from whom it came in the first place. This profound interchange of love now bears fruit in all that they say and do, for the world that God is now able to reach through them. Saint Francis was in theory a mystic because he saw so clearly, and stated so emphatically, that all true virtue and all genuine goodness is in God and in God alone, and can only enter into Man through a mystic death to the 'Old Man' who prevents the 'New Man' from being formed. He was a practical mystic also because he continually sought out the solitary environment necessary in which to enable the Holy Spirit to bring about this mystic death with a shaft of light and life that contained all the virtues and all the gifts that have their spiritual origin in God, and their physical manifestation in Man — the Christ-like Man.

"'The sure sign for Francis that what appears as true virtue is not its counterfeit, is that it is never alone, for if it is born of the love of God from within, it is born into a whole family of virtues that appear simultaneously, if gradually, in the behavior of the true believer. In other words, if you meet a tolerant person who is a glutton, or a generous person who is a tyrant, or a patient person who is a swindler, then the virtue that might seem to redeem them is only of human origin, and born of the genes they inherited, or the upbringing that others gave them, or the expediency that social acceptance demands of them, as your own Jane Austen saw so incisively.

"'It is only as weak human love is suffused and surcharged

141

by the divine, that a believer is now able to love God with their whole heart and with their whole mind and with their whole strength, and to love their neighbor as themselves, and so keep all the commandments, that a promise can be kept. The promise was made by Christ Himself at the Last Supper, when He promised that whosoever keeps these commandments would be loved in such a way that the Father, the Son and the Holy Spirit would make a home within them so that the community of God's own life can dwell on earth in the person who is redeemed by love.

'"As this whole process of transformation, or divinization, is taking place, the mystic begins to experience the love that they are receiving, sometimes to shattering degrees of intensity, and with a regularity that finally becomes permanent, as the Trinity of love which is God is finally 'homed' within them for good. This is true contemplation, a pure gift of God, that cannot be generated by any man-made methods or techniques from the East or from the West. Those who suggest otherwise are simply deceiving you, as they have been deceived themselves.

'"It is a tangible experiential knowledge from which strength is drawn that enables the mystic to sever themselves from all and everything that prevents them living to the full the Christ-life, that enables them to live fully for others. In the authentic mystic you will always find a fully balanced and complete person who is not so lost in a self-indulgent evangelical piety that they forget the physical needs of others, nor so engrossed in their socio-political involvement that they forget the spiritual needs of themselves.

'"Two priorities are always embodied simultaneously in the true mystic — love of God and love of Man. See how the theological and the sociological are completely harmonized in the life of Jesus Christ, the greatest mystic ever to walk on the face of this earth. He was totally open and available to everyone because He was first totally available to God. If He hadn't received in the desert or on the mountainside, in lonely places, in the inner room or in the Garden of Gethsemane, then He would have nothing to give by the lake side at the crossroads, in the marketplace, the synagogue, the Temple precincts, or the place of execution where He gave His all.

"'Jesus knew this, and stated it so clearly that the true disciples who have followed Him throughout the ages heard Him, and they followed the example that He gave. Francis may well have been a mystic of the highest order, and spent years of his life in solitary prayer, but what other man in the whole of the Middle Ages did more for his fellow men than did he? for the poor with whom he worked? for the lepers he served with his own hands? and for the peace he brought to the strife-stricken world in which he lived? Look at my own spiritual director, Padre Pio, a mystic who has scaled the heights, a healer, a miracle worker of almost unprecedented stature, and yet sixteen hours a day, sometimes more, he gives himself in humble service to his fellow man. See for yourself the hospital he is building to give work to the unemployed in Southern Italy and the medical help that has been denied them for so long by a government more interested in votes, than in the misery of their voters.

"'But I've said enough for one day, Peter, let me just finish by giving you the second law of thermodynamics which is this: a cold body cannot communicate heat to a hotter body. Once again Francis and other faithful followers of Christ knew this principle long before science formulated it — for this is why Francis went to the cave, so that his body could be set alight with a fire that would kindle others. This is why I am here, Peter, and this is why you too must seek out solitude as a true Franciscan to be first purified by the fire of the Holy Spirit, so that in His name you can be set afire with a love that you must in your way, but in God's time, communicate to others.

"'I am here, waiting upon God as best I can. I will wait here till death if that is what is required of me, or I will leave tomorrow morning if something else is required of me, to help build up the Brotherhood of Man on earth, which is the deepest desire of any true follower of Francis of Assisi."

'At last I had found someone to whom I could really talk at

Monte Casale, literally a man after my own heart, for the life he was living was exactly the life that I had been aspiring to myself before other considerations had blurred my vision. I returned to speak with Antonio every day in the few remaining weeks that were left to me before I was due to leave for Paris and my profession. I learnt so many practical things from him that would help me later when I finally settled on Calvay, and so many other truths about the spiritual journey that have sustained me to this day. I was fascinated to hear from him that Monte Casale had been a Third Order hermitage for several centuries after the death of Saint Francis, and before the coming of the Capuchins in the middle of the sixteenth century.

'Antonio also told me not just that Francis had written a rule for hermits, but that he had written it while living the life of a hermit himself, here at Monte Casale, and he promised to give me a copy of the text to take away with me. However, it would be untrue to pretend that my newfound friendship with Antonio, and the help he had given me, healed the gaping wounds that had been opened in my heart — they were deep, very deep, and they bled profusely especially at those times when, with Antonio's encouragement, I sought out the solitary prayer that I had been avoiding.

'One phrase in the letter Françoise had written to me began to haunt me in and out of prayer, because it held out to me some hope, not of what I'd hoped for before, but because it held out to me the possibility of a new start with the security that comes from knowing that you are loved, even though needs must distance that love from where I'd wish it. She had said, referring to a time when we might once more write to one another "...when time may well have tempered the mutual feelings that make it imperative for us both to pursue our different vocations without any further personal relationship." It was the phrase "mutual feelings" that kept my mind turning over and over, and my memory desperately tried to recall any word or action that could lead me to believe, or even hope, that there could be in her even the slightest flicker of love to match the flame that was in me.

'I could not write to her for my letters would be returned unopened. I couldn't visit her either for she would not see me, so at least the desire to know the answer to the question that endlessly rose up to haunt me, led me back to prayer. I prayed with a fervor I'd not known for months for some sign that would quiet my mind, and enable me to go forward upon the way, secure in the knowledge that I was loved, with the love of the only one whose love mattered to me.

'I had just got up from my siesta on the Sunday before I was due to return to Paris when Antonio burst excitedly into my room, apologizing for the intrusion.

"'I've got some fantastic news," he said.

"'Oh," I said rather coolly, knowing that there was only one piece of fantastic news that would interest me, and I knew it was not that. "What is it?" I said.

"'Padre Bernadino is going to his sister's wedding tomorrow morning, and the wedding is to be held in his home town, San Marco in Lamis, this Wednesday."

'I couldn't help but laugh. "But I don't see why you're so excited about it, nor what it has got to do with me."

"'Well," he said, "San Marco is a little village in Southern Italy, only a few miles away from San Giovanni Rotondo, and Padre Bernadino said you could go with him if you'd like to meet Padre Pio."

"'Oh, I see," I said, frankly unmoved. To be honest, I didn't care a fig about seeing Padre Pio, saint or no saint. I had other things on my mind of far greater moment to me on the eve of my departure from Monte Casale.

'I still had hopes, like my good friend Micawber, that something would turn up before I had to leave on the following Thursday. I still counted the seconds during my morning meditation to the time when the postman would leave his daily parcel of post. I still hoped that Padre Angelo would suddenly decide it was time to visit Clitunno again and take me with him. To commit myself to some sort of wild goose chase, just to see some supposed saint when something might yet turn up, didn't appeal to me at all.

145

'Antonio hadn't noticed my reluctance, because he was so excited about the great opportunity that had suddenly presented itself.

'"It's an answer to a prayer," he said, "because I, myself, am desperate for Padre Pio's advice; Padre Angelo wants me to become the spiritual director to the Third Order here in Borgo San Sepolcro, and I wouldn't think of taking such a step without the advice of my spiritual director. Will you please give him this letter and tell him it's urgent?"

'"Yes, of course," I said as Antonio thrust the letter into my hand, realizing that the very words I uttered, without time for serious thought, had committed me to the journey that I frankly didn't want to make.

'"Padre Bernadino has been given the car until next Friday so he'll be able to drop you at the airport before he returns here later that day. Now he said he's leaving at the crack of dawn, because he has things to do in Rome before driving south on Tuesday morning. He said he'll make all the arrangements, so you'll have somewhere to stay. He knows everyone there is to know at San Giovanni Rotondo."

'It was with a very sad and sore heart that I set off at first light, speeding down the narrow mountain road on our way to Borgo San Sepolcro, where we'd meet the main highway. Just before we reached the bottom, I saw the postman on his way up, and motioned desperately to Dino to pull in. There were two letters for me and one for Dino. One of my letters was from home, the other was from Madame de Gaye to inform me that Père Claude was coming down from Lyon to preside at my profession and that she had been given permission to have the ceremony in her private chapel as I had requested.

'Dino whooped with delight at the contents of his letter. It was confirmation that there would be a ticket awaiting his arrival in Rome for the European Cup Match between Roma and Real Madrid — it was apparently the semi-final. There was no stopping him after that. He drove like a madman toward the eternal city, and the eternal football stadium that was for him the nearest thing to heaven this side of the grave.

'My heart started pounding as we passed Trevi, and drew closer and closer to Clitunno. I was desperate to stop, if only for a few minutes, just to be near the place where the person I loved more than anyone else in the world lived and breathed — just to breathe the same air for a few moments was all that I asked.

'"Could you stop for a few minutes at Fonti del Clitunno, Dino?" I said. "I've passed the place several times but never seen it."

'"Sure," said Dino. "It'll give me the opportunity to have a fag and stretch my legs."

'He was quite chatty when we got out of the car, and began explaining why the source of the Clitumnus meant so much to his forebears, the Roman soldiers who conquered the ancient world.

'"You see, they believed that the Clitumnus would do for them what the mythical River Styx could do for the Greeks. Once they bathed in these waters they thought they would be made invulnerable in battle."

'"It's certainly got atmosphere," I said. And it had. The waters were so still and so clear, and the surrounding banks so lush and laden with willows, bent low to see their own reflection in the waters; and the poplars stood tall and erect like the soldiers, dead long since, who'd bathed in the sacred waters.

'"There seems to be no movement at all," I said, "and yet the water must be moving to supply the great river that flows out of it."

'"Yes," he said, "the water collects from the limestone mountains up there, behind us, and then it seeps up through the silt from under the Flaminian Way, that we have just been traveling on."

'As he directed my gaze to the mountains above, I was delighted to look upwards, not to the heights but to the little tell-tale tower of rough brickwork, which was the highest point of the little eremo, where I would far rather have been. Oh, for the wings of a dove, I thought.

'Dino was still rabbiting on about the poets who had visited the spot and who'd been so inspired by the clarity, the stillness and the purity of the sacred waters. I vaguely heard him mention the name of Virgil among a list of other poets whom I had never heard of before — my mind was elsewhere.

"'Your own Byron came here, too, and it even moved him to song," said Dino, taking me by the arm and leading me back to the car.

"'I was just looking at the eremo," I said. "You can see it just sticking out above the trees."

"'Oh, that confounded place," he said. "What on earth did they decide to build a convent in that outlandish spot for. It's a damn nuisance. I've got to trek all the way up there on my way back, just to pick up Angelo's sermon book, that he left there after his last visit."

"'Really," I said, trying to keep at least an outward calm as my mind sprang into action to try and exploit the possibility, that I never thought would have presented itself — it was only an outside chance, but even an outside chance is better than none at all.

"'Why not pop up now?" I said as casually as I could, "and get it over with. We've got time on our hands and I wouldn't mind going up with you. It would give me the opportunity to make my farewells to the Sisters. They've been very good to me."

"'No," said Dino. "I want to get to hell out of this backwater and get to civilization as soon as possible."

"'O.K." I said, as we both got back into the car. "I just thought," I said, as he turned on the ignition, "that it would have given you a few extra hours in Perugia on your way back." It was my trump card, but was it high enough? I quickly looked away, so that he could make the necessary calculations in his mind without him feeling I was in any way aware of the lure that I had laid before him.

"'Well," he said, looking at his watch. "Time is on our side, so if you'd really like to make your farewells it would kill two birds with one stone."

'I felt ashamed at what I'd done, but the truth of the matter was I would have done anything to make the visit that I thought I may never make again.

'The Superior was decidedly cool towards both of us. She gave Dino Father Angelo's sermon book, but was quite adamant that Sister Françoise was busy in the garden when I asked to see her.

'"It's just for a few minutes," I said.

'"Sorry," she said. "Perhaps if it was after supper at the permitted time it might just be possible, but not at this time of the day"

'Dino had already told her that we were in a hurry to get to Rome, so she was on safe ground.

'"Look, Sister, it's important, very important," I said, pleading. I took a letter out of my pocket — "I received this letter only two hours ago from her mother, with a message in it for her. It's important."

'Reluctantly she turned and disappeared along the corridor. She was back in a few minutes. "Sister Françoise said she can't possibly come, but she said if it's an important message you can leave it with me."

'I was shattered, but I still had to act as normally as I could even though the message I had to leave hardly merited the urgency with which I had announced it.

'"Oh, it's to say that my profession will be on Easter Tuesday at twelve o'clock," I said lamely, though I did try to inject into my works the importance that the news did merit, at least for me.

'"I see," said the Superior. She smiled with her mouth but not with her eyes. "I'm sure we will all remember you in our prayers."

'As if all that wasn't embarrassing enough, Dino started to bait me on the way down. "Well, well, Peter," he said. "You're a dark horse. So it was our Aphrodite that you wanted to see after all."

'I was furious, not because he compared Françoise to the beautiful goddess of love, but because he had the impertinence to refer to her as "our" Aphrodite, as if he had some sort of claim on her.

'"Take my advice," he said. "You'll get nowhere with Miss High-and-Mighty. She's got too big an idea of herself, just because she's supposed to have blue blood in her veins. She thinks she's a cut above the rest. I'll bring her down to size one of these fine days."

'I was blazing, and it showed.

'"Oh, Peter," he said. "I see you're blushing. Now I know why you've been haunting the postman for the last four months."

'I wasn't blushing with embarrassment. It was anger that crimsoned my face; an anger that would have made me hit him in the eye there and then had some unseen hand not restrained me. I was glad when I was alone again in my room at the friary while he went off to his precious match, even though I had nothing to do. I sat there for hours on end like a masochist, whiling away the time, picking and prodding the new wounds that had once again opened up a heart already scarred enough from the ravages of love lost and never to be regained.

'Five miles out of Rome Dino stopped the car. He took off his habit to reveal the Teddy-boy outfit that he usually reserved for clandestine visits to Perugia.

'"That's better," he said as he settled back into the driving seat, lighting up a cigarette to settle his nerves for the nerve-racking journey ahead.

'Thank God that Roma won 3-2 in extra time, I thought. That was a small mercy that made the very long journey south at least a little less unbearable.

'Dino raised the town from its usual torpor, when he hooted his way around the streets that had raised him, and waved at almost everyone who seemed genuinely pleased to see the prodigal's return. He didn't stop however, but drove straight to San Giovanni Rotondo, where true to form he hadn't made any arrangements for me to stay at the friary, or anywhere else for that matter, and only managed to find me a bed for the night because his third cousin once removed didn't dare deny the demands of her illustrious relative from Rome. He only waited long enough to say he'd pick me up again at seven thirty sharp on the Thursday morning for the long journey back to Rome, leaving me a full day to while away the time in a dead and alive little Italian backwater.

'"No," I said, "I would not be getting up at five o'clock to go to the Padre's Mass. I'd be having a long lie-in." I thought I deserved it, and I had no intention of getting up in the middle of the night to go to the Padre's Mass. After all, it was the same Mass whoever said it.

'As it happened I went to the ten o'clock Mass after the long sleep and the delicious Italian breakfast that kept me going all day. I stayed on to pray in the church after Mass and I prayed once again with a fervor that leapt upwards from my heart to a God with whom I pleaded for a sign, some sign, any sign that, despite the events of that previous morning, Françoise harbored at least some love in her heart for the man who felt his life was meaningless without it.

'I was continually disturbed by several dozen men who kept moving up, a place at a time, as one of their number went into the sacristy, presumably for confession, presumably to Padre — whatever his name was, who Antonio wanted me to see. Frankly, I'd no desire to see him because, quite apart from anything else, I'd no desire to pour out the story of my life all over again, and anyway I would not, definitely not, talk to another living soul about my relationship with my very dear Françoise. It was my business and mine alone.

'I was almost in tears, lost in self-pity, when I was tapped on the shoulder by a heavily-built man with dark glasses, who looked as if he were the resident god-father's right-hand man. "Padre will see you now," he said.

'"Padre who?" I said.

'"Padre Pio, of course," he said. "Come quickly."

'"Wait a minute," I said, pulling my arm away from his. "There is some mistake. I've made no appointment to see him."

'"Well, he wants to see you," came the reply. "Come."

'Once again I pulled my arm away. "How do you know it's me he wants to see?"

'"He said go and tell the young Englishman with the stick and the built-up boot that I would like to see him."

'I quickly glanced round, not really expecting to find many more men in the church who answered that description. Before I could make any more queries, I was on my feet thanks to the messenger of light, who looked as if he'd just come from outer darkness. He closed the door behind me as I was ushered into the sacristy where apparently it was the Padre's custom to hear the men's confessions.

'It took me months afterwards to try and transpose into words the immediate impact of that first meeting with a man I now know to be a living saint. The preoccupation with my own affairs had made me quite unprepared for that brief meeting, which was to have such a deep effect upon my life.

'When I first met Françoise I immediately felt at home because I knew instinctively that we shared the same ideas and ideals; the same hopes and aspirations. I had a similar feeling the moment my eyes fell upon the man who turned to greet me as I walked into the sacristy, only this time the ideas and ideals, the hopes and aspirations that Françoise and I had in common, were in him completely fulfilled. His face was a friendly fusion of all the rare gifts and qualities that reflect the human spirit at its most endearing. Years of suffering had fathered a profound sense of peace and joy that determined the very texture of his demeanor. It was most evident in his eyes, where it had been softened into compassion. There was a most innocent and guileless goodness that expressed itself in a humble, child-like humor, that played around the lips and gave to the eyes a brightness that completed the compassion with a hope that must have spoken to so many, who were sowing in tears, of the day when they would reap in joy.

'He welcomed me like an elder brother, not as a Padre. He took both my hands in his, and helped me into the seat opposite his own. I knew instinctively that I did not need to tell him my story for he already knew it, with a knowledge that comes from a love that could see at a glance, what others could never see in a lifetime.

'My belief in reincarnation dates from that meeting; not the reincarnation of every man, but of the perfect Man, who makes himself flesh again in as many different ways as there are those who would receive Him.

'"Your prayer has been answered," he said simply, "and the sign you seek will be given to support you on the journey that you are preparing to undertake. God has called you to become a prophet, Peter. It is a great gift, a great privilege, but it carries with it a great and grave responsibility. A prophet must speak to a world who would rather not hear the message that he brings. All prophets have first to be purified themselves before they can help purify others.

'"Like the One you wish to follow, you must spend many hidden years away from the eyes of man, many years in the desert, where all the prophets are prepared to return to the world of Man with a message from God. One day in God's good time, not yours, when He thinks you're ready, not when you do, there is a work for you to perform in Man's world, that will be a sign that God's world is close. God will do His part if you do yours, and your part is to pray, trust and not worry."

'He said many other things to me that are too personal to tell, although I must have been with him no more than twenty minutes. I begged him to pray for me, and he promised he always would as he always did for those he adopted as his spiritual sons.

'Just before I turned to go he said, "Haven't you got something for me?"

'I looked blank.

'"Antonio's letter," he said with a broad grin.

'"Oh yes, of course," I said. I put my hand into the inside pocket of my jacket, and gave him the letter that he couldn't possibly have known that I had brought.

'I have heard the expression "walking on air" but I had never experienced it until that day. It was as if I was several inches off the ground, as I made my way back to my place in the church. Apart from certain things he said to me about my future, which are personal and private, he said nothing that I hadn't heard before, or would hear in the future. In fact, I'd heard and would hear more profound truths about the spiritual life explained at length, but never again would I receive what I received from him. He was a true apostle, and so when he spoke, he spoke with a power that came from within, that not only gave the words that he spoke a depth of meaning far deeper than the mind alone can grasp, but a power too, that strengthened you to do the word that was spoken to you.

'The moment I knelt in prayer I was totally absorbed in God, in such a way that I had no distractions at all, and then all of a sudden the same prayer that had raised me up in Notre Dame raised me up again. It was as if I spiraled upwards once more in the higher part of my head to the same degree of intensity that I experienced then, only now it lasted longer than before, and I remained riveted to the spot, quite oblivious of what was going on around me for longer than I will ever know. Time no longer seemed to have any meaning any more. When there are no longer any distractions or temptations, or any thoughts of any kind, when there are no "befores or afters" there's no means of calculating time.

'The high mystical peaks that I was raised to experience, subsided at times to plateaus where the absorption was not so completely all-engrossing. Then, without warning, I would spiral upwards again to peaks that had been scaled before, as the power of God tangibly worked within me without any effort on my part, for I was totally in God's hands, and happy to be so. All the trials and the sufferings I had been through over the last few months seemed as nothing, and I would willingly have undergone them all ten times over for the love that I received in that sublime prayer.

'As before, the experience made me feel humble, not proud,

aware of my own nothingness, and of the greatness of God that made me realize that once possessed by His power nothing would be impossible to me, or rather to the new me, part human, part divine.

'When I stood up to leave the church, I felt unsteady on my feet, as if slightly inebriated with what I had received. I felt taller, too, as I looked down to the ground, but my feet were firmly grounded, and the experience soon faded with the feeling of unsteadiness as I went outside; but the feeling of inebriation remained with me for several days.

'I don't remember much about the rest of that day. I just remember walking around the streets of San Giovanni Rotondo as if in a daze, as if I were in a dream, still engrossed in God, but with an absorption that did not prevent me from moving, as I had been unable to move in the church. After waiting for an hour for Dino to turn up, I went to pray in the church the following morning, leaving a message that he could pick me up there. I was still experiencing an absorption in God that made me aware of His abiding presence within me, and all about me.

'It was about nine o'clock when I turned round, distracted by a commotion at the back of the church, to see the arrival of Dino who was greeting and being greeted by half a dozen villagers, who obviously recognized the local lad who they thought had made good. I got up to join the happy throng. Just as I was reaching them a young Brother came out of a side door and said, "Oh, by the way, Bernadino, you're wanted for a moment in the sacristy."

'"OK kiddo," he said, patronizing the young man, and he set off with his own inimitable gait up the side aisle, with his Teddy-boy trousers hanging down beneath his habit. He made a perfunctory genuflection and waltzed into the sacristy with simply no idea what, or rather who, awaited him. The funny thing is I knew exactly what was going to happen, though I didn't know how long it would take. After all, I'd never witnessed a miracle before. It's comparatively easy to cure cripples; it doesn't take too long to give hearing back to the deaf or sight to the blind, that is if you happen to be a Padre Pio. But even for him, prodigal sons take a bit longer, quite a bit longer if they happen to be a Bernadino of Perugia.

'It was half an hour before the sacristy door opened again and Dino emerged. It was not a new man I saw; it takes many years to make a new man, but it was a different man, a very different man. The man who went in was a man full of himself, intoxicated with his own importance, thirsting with desires and urges that he couldn't resist. But it was a sober man who came out, who would never be quite the same again, though he hardly knew it himself at the time. He hadn't had time to adjust to what had happened, hadn't had time to come to terms with the new direction that his life was about to take, so he tried to act as casually as he could, to play for the time he needed, for the reflection that the sudden and unexpected interview called for, and for the adjustment that had to be made. After all, it was to change the life of a man no one else had thought was changeable.

'He made some remark about having to pick up a letter from Padre Pio for Antonio, but he said no more, nor did I press him for I had no right to pry into his privacy any more than he had to pry into mine. Dino gave no verbal indication that anything unusual or extraordinary had happened in that meeting with Padre Pio, until he dropped me at the airport early the next morning. He wanted to come to see me off, but I insisted that he should leave me because he had a long journey ahead of him.

'"It will take you at least five hours to get to Perugia," I said.

'"I won't be going to Perugia," he answered. "Not now, not ever." Then he jumped out of the car and embraced me "Italian style." "Forgive me, Peter," he said. "I must have been a great source of scandal to you. Please forgive me and pray for me. It's about time I grew up. I'm going back to Monte Casale, and I'll stay there, too, because I want to start anew. I want to begin my life all over again."

'I didn't need to think of what to say or how to react because before I knew what was happening, he was back in the car again and he'd gone; gone to begin a new life he should have started years ago, but at least he'd started now thanks to the man who'd done for both of us what he did for so many every day of his life.

'Ten years later I heard that Padre Bernadino had been made Novice Master and turned out to be one of the best they'd ever had.

'I spent Holy Week at Citeaux, preparing myself for my profession on Easter Tuesday, then I returned to Rue de Magdebourg on the Monday to hear that Père La Bec and Anton, and my brother David would be coming for my profession the following day. Robert knocked at my door the next morning shortly after breakfast and brought in a pile of post. I shouldn't have opened it until after the profession, but I'd never been able to resist opening letters the moment they arrived. I had no idea so many people knew about my profession day. There was a card from home, from my brother Tony, from Boris, from Padre Angelo and Antonio, and would you believe it, from Father Dimitrius. I suppose Boris must have told him.

'I was still reading the long letter from Antonio when Robert knocked at the door again. "Oh M'sieur Pierre, forgive me, I forgot to give you this. It arrived last Saturday." He handed me a small parcel. Strangely, I didn't recognize the writing, for I should have. I turned it over and there on the back were two words "Eremo Clitunno." I ripped the parcel open like a hungry animal and tore open the letter that was inside it.

'"Please, please forgive me," were the first words I read. "Please, please forgive me for not seeing you last week but I simply couldn't. Before you visited me from Montefalco my mother had written to me to tell me that you had undoubtedly fallen in love with me, and she begged me to respect the vocation that she is sure that you have. I found it hard to believe that you did love me, but I nevertheless promised her that I would do nothing to encourage you in any way to give up the special vocation that I, too, believe you have been called to. I also told her that if I thought it necessary I would even tell you about my sordid past, and the slut that I have been, and still am for that matter, so that any illusions you may have about me would be smashed.

'"The week after I had written to you for the last time, I had a letter from my mother telling me that you already knew about my past, and had known about it before we ever met. This news shattered me, to think that in the full knowledge of what I had been, and what I am, you still not only loved me but wanted to spend your life with me. I simply couldn't cope with it all, and I spoke to my Superior and told her everything. If it had not been for her I would have left to join my life with yours so that we could seek God together in the way I know you wanted to propose to me had things turned out differently.

'"In spite of her help and understanding, I know without a shadow of a doubt that had I come to see you on your last visit I would have packed my bags and come with you no matter what the consequences. Deep down I know now that I did the right thing in refusing to see you though it still breaks my heart every time I think about it. Please accept the small gift I've enclosed for you. It might not seem much but it's very dear to me and I want you to have it, to wear it as a sign of our mutual love that will never keep us apart, except by the distance that love can always span.

'"God bless you always, Peter.

'"All my love for ever and ever, and even longer.

'"Françoise."

'I put the letter down and opened the gift that was wrapped in a small piece of tissue paper. To my surprise it was a small piece of string, or rather cord, with three knots in it. Then it suddenly struck me what it was, and why it meant so much to Françoise. It was the cord given to her by the saintly old dear who had changed her life, and now she was giving it to me. I knew how much that cord meant to her, and the love that giving it to me symbolized. I would wear it for my profession and continually, to remind me of the bond that united us together, and the common way of life to which we had both committed ourselves.

'Padre Pio was right. My prayer would be, had been,

answered and more than answered, for the letter said much more than I had ever hoped for. Now at last I was ready for the profession that I was about to make, and for the journey that I was going to start. I felt surrounded and supported by more love than I could ever hope for, from my family, from my friends, from all those good men and women who had helped me over the past few years, and most of all from my very dear Françoise, who will always be in my heart as I will be in hers, so that together we can open our hearts to the only One for Whom we both live, and to Whom we have both committed our lives.'

* * * * * * * * * *

It was almost one thirty when I had finished the enthralling story of Peter's last few months in Italy, his meeting with Padre Pio, and of the human love that had no doubt supported him to this day. The typescript had so excited me that I simply couldn't get to sleep, and then all of a sudden a thought struck me, and I leapt out of bed and rushed over to the filing cabinet. If Françoise had written to him when she promised then the letter, or maybe the letters, would be somewhere there. I began furiously searching everywhere, until finally at the back of the last drawer I saw a large file with a small tab sticking up on top of it with the name "Françoise" written clearly upon it.

I pulled it out and rushed back to bed to find not just the letter but letters, many letters, that Peter had received from Françoise over the last ten years or more, but to my great disappointment they were, of course, all written in French. No matter how great my excitement or how desperate I was to read them, my French is not what it was, and it never was what it should have been, so I had to put the file back into the cabinet, at least until the next day when, with my little grey cells recharged and the help of a good French dictionary, I would be able to decipher the letters that I desperately wanted to read.

I had been so excited by what I had read and by the prospect

159

of what I was going to read the next day that I simply couldn't sleep, so finally I took a sleeping pill I kept for emergency purposes to make sure that I made full use of what was left of the day ahead. It was that pill that ensured that I was in a deep, deep sleep when I heard an incessant banging coming from some level of consciousness that I couldn't at first identify. I slumbered on for a while in a state of semi-oblivion until suddenly I realized it was my door. In that same moment I began to feel the strange unworthy feelings coming over me as once more I began to identify myself with Angus MacNeil, and the sound of the door with Beatson and his constables. The sudden recollection of what had followed before, jolted me into immediate action and I sprang to my feet, determined to confront the intruders, this time man to man.

What the hell if I was only wearing my pajama trousers, I thought, as I grabbed the carving knife from the breadboard, and made for the door with all the male fury I could muster.

"I'm not bloody deaf," I roared as I unbolted the door, cutting my hand in the process. "For God's sake," I shouted as I swung the door open.

I think it was the cold morning air that finally woke me up, and jerked me back into the world of reality. Reality presented herself to me that unforgettable morning in the form of Mother Superior from the convent, and two novices, who had accompanied her. Not even the pains and purifications of purgatory, if I ever get there, will wipe away the memory of that awful moment. There I stood, hardly more than a naked, hairy chest thrust out to bar the intruders' way, with an aggressive ape-like expression on my face to deter even the most determined intruder. I blush to this day when I think of the final touch: a vicious-looking carving knife, dripping with blood, half raised and ready for action.

One of the novices turned and fled down the path. The second rushed forward like a little child to snuggle for security into the folds of her Superior's ample form. She, for her part, turned like Lot's wife to salt and stood her ground because she couldn't move from it. If Perseus had ever seen the face of Medusa, would it have been a more horrendous sight than the sight I saw? It turned me to stone on the spot, and I may have been there still had the knife not fallen from my grasp and homed itself into my heel. Did Achilles roar as I roared? Did he swear as I swore? Did he utter such terrible oaths as I uttered, so unspeakable that they must remain unspoken until the end of time?

The "human touch" broke the spell that had petrified all three of us. "Sorry! Sorry!" the poor woman shouted as she began to shake all over on her way back to normality. "We were told there was a Catholic priest, who was staying here."

I don't know how long she had to wait for a response because I was quite unable to react. I just remember hearing words unwillingly making their way out of my mouth, though I didn't identify with them at the time.

"I-am-that-Catholic-priest-I-am-Father-Robertson, Father James Robertson."

It was probably the word "Father" that did it — touched something deep down in the child's unconscious, for the young novice suddenly loosened her grip on her spiritual mother and gazed at me with all simplicity and innocence, and said,

"Then you must come quickly for Peter is due to arrive at Castlebay within the hour."

From then on things happened so fast that I hadn't time to reflect on that horrendous incident that made the humiliation I'd suffered only a few days before seem as nothing. Only one thought haunted me as I dressed, more quickly than I had ever dressed before, for I knew that once explained all would be forgiven, and the story of my humiliation would be told and re-told around many a holy hearth.

But those oaths I had uttered. That unspeakable language I had spoken. Would they be forgotten or forgiven? Perhaps not, I thought, as I put on my dog-collar, but at least, they'll never be repeated. No, not this side of the eternal tape-recorder. That's for sure.

8

Not a word was said on the short voyage back to the mainland about the embarrassing incident that had just happened.

I couldn't believe my eyes, as I made my way towards the house from the jetty — Father James had just arrived with Peter from Castlebay. They were immediately surrounded by a group of Islanders, and the happy throng poured into the presbytery.

Was I still dreaming, I thought. Could it really be true? Was that really Peter?

Apparently Father James's housekeeper had received a phone call the night before to say that Peter was alive and well, and would be arriving on the early morning ferry from Oban. Naturally it was too late to inform me, so the Sisters had been despatched at first light.

The celebrations went on all day and Peter told and retold his story as each new batch of visitors arrived and what a story it was. It seemed he'd had some sort of heart attack that had left him prostrate in his little boat. He may well have died had a large Russian trawler with a doctor on board not picked him up in the Minch.

As the trawler was carrying some compromising equipment the Captain was not allowed to put in to any foreign port, for any reason whatsoever, so Peter had been taken back to Russia. He was in hospital for over a month before he was considered fit enough to be sent home.

He then had to spend ten days in London being debriefed

by officials from the Ministry of Defense, because Peter's fluent Russian had enabled him to pick up a good deal of information that was considered invaluable. The Naval raiding party, who'd put the fear of God into me a few days before, had been sent by the M.O.D. to check up on Peter's background.

Peter insisted that I should stay on Calvay, and spend the night with him, and I was delighted to accept his invitation, to hear from him more details of his adventures. He was too tired however, and so was I for that matter, so we both went straight to bed. It was mid morning before Peter emerged and we both sat round the kitchen table for breakfast. Peter had found his ordeal horrific, not because of his heart condition, but because of the horrors of nuclear war, that he had learned about from both sides of the iron curtain.

"You see," said Peter, "I discovered that the trawler I was on was a floating communications center linking a whole fleet of submarines carrying nuclear missiles, that could obliterate the whole country in a matter of minutes. The missiles could be fired off at such short range that no early warning system would ever be able to prevent them.

"I'm afraid it's all been too much for me," said Peter. "Here we are at the end of the twentieth century when man has supposedly come of age, and the most highly developed nations on earth are busily employed in plotting how to bomb and burn one another off the face of the earth, and people say hell fire is only metaphorical language!

"I'm afraid the 'brave new world' man has been trying to make for himself depends on a whole pseudo-philosophy of power-seeking and greed that has fundamentally corrupted what once were genuine human ideals.

"If the very existence of the bomb doesn't make people see the moral morass that we are all in — then they will never see! It's not just the bomb, but what the bomb signifies."

"Do you really think that man is worse today than ever before?" I asked. "Or is it just that modern communications have made us more aware of what man has always been like in the past?"

"It's a popular debating point," said Peter. "But what is not debatable is that for the first time man has at his fingertips the buttons that can blow up the world up to ten times over.

"I don't want to play the prophet of doom, but I am quite convinced that whether by accident or design man will blow himself to smithereens unless he is radically changed, not by politics but by religion.

"Politics is only the art of the possible — religion is the art of the impossible.

"This is why I keep emphasizing prayer, not because prayer changes God's heart, but because it changes man's heart. Only in this way will human beings be changed from the inside, so that they can live safely and in peace with one another.

"However, don't get me going on that theme, or I'll go on all day, and I'm afraid I must be leaving now."

"Oh no!" I said, horrified that the chat I was so looking forward to was going to end before it had even started.

"I'm so sorry," said Peter, "but I have to leave in a few minutes — I've got to leave for an appointment with my doctor at the hospital on South Uist, and then I have to pick up my boat from Eriskay."

"Oh dear," I said, "I was looking forward to spending the afternoon with you to hear more about your stay in Russia."

"I'm so sorry," said Peter, "but there'll be plenty of time next month, when I presume you'll be coming as we'd planned before all this happened."

"Oh yes," I said, "I certainly will."

"I'll tell you more about Russia then — there's so much to tell. I was terribly impressed by all that I experienced in hospital. I may have given the impression that I think the Russians are 'baddies' and we in the West are the 'goodies' — if I have then I've certainly given you the wrong impression. The people at the top may arguably be worse than the people at the top in the so-called 'free world' but in many respects they are as bad as one another.

"What impressed me was the faith of the ordinary people in Russia who've suffered so much. I met countless numbers of Christians when I was in hospital, who risked their jobs, their livelihoods and much more, just to pray for me by my bedside, or press a crucifix into my hands, or some other token of our common faith.

"On one occasion in the middle of the night a group of Christians dressed as doctors and nurses pulled screens around my bed, and one of their number, a priest, gave me the Sacrament of the Sick.

"Four of them including the priest were wearing the 'Tau.'"

"What's that," I asked.

"Well, it's a T-shaped cross that Saint Francis used as part of his signature, and it is worn today by members of his Third Order all over the world as a sign of their Franciscan calling.

"You see," said Peter, "I'm a member of the Third Order of Saint Francis and they knew that I belonged to the same family."

"How did they know that?"

"Well, one of the nurses discovered that I was wearing a Third Order cord under my clothing, and she must have passed the word on. I always wear it. It was given to me by a very dear friend many years ago, and I've worn it since my profession day."

I was dying to say something but I managed to keep my mouth shut.

"When you come out here next month I'll tell you more about my experiences in Russia, and we'll have more time to speak about other things too, but I think I'd better be making a move now."

Suddenly the presence of Peter did something to me, although he hadn't specifically been speaking about the spiritual life.

It's strange how the presence of pure goodness in another brings out the child in you.

"Peter, I've failed so often since we last met," I blurted out, "but I'm going to start again with your help."

"Well," said Peter, with a reassuring smile. "If you say you've failed so many times it must mean that you have continually started trying again, and in the Trying is the Dying; the dying to the 'Old Man,' the egotist within you, so that the 'New Man' can be born. You can do no more than try, inside or outside of prayer. Every moment is a moment for Trying, for Dying, and for Rising till Christ be perfectly formed within you. Simone Weil once said a person is no more than the quality of their endeavor. This is how God will judge us all. Not by what we have achieved; not by some man-made measure of success, but by how best we have tried.

"When the final trumpet sounds, God won't say 'What interior mansion were you in or what rung of the ladder of perfection were you on,' but 'How best did you try?' Believe me, the whole of the spiritual life, the very essence of mystical prayer is about Dying through Trying. It is not the cowards, it is the saints who die a thousand times before their death, and it is in this Dying, through this Trying that they reach the height of the spiritual life: total identity, complete at-one-ment with the Christ of Easter Day."

"That's something I'd like to ask you about," I said, "now that you've mentioned it."

"What?" said Peter.

"Mystical prayer."

"I'm afraid that's a subject that would keep us talking into the small hours of tomorrow week. But," he said, "we will talk about it at another time; at the right time, when the time is right for you, and that's not now.

"I'm afraid you must excuse me. I must leave for Uist without delay. I'll see you at the plane tomorrow morning." And with that, he left me. He left me a little disappointed and just a little hurt.

That afternoon I moved back into the presbytery, to spend the night in the room where I'd slept before I went out to Calvay. I knew Peter would appreciate the privacy, and it would make it easier for me to get the plane home the next morning. I stayed up late talking to Father James, so it was almost midnight before I got to bed, and we had to be up before sunrise.

If I'd fallen asleep immediately I don't think I would have noticed it, but I didn't, and so I did. The smell I mean. It was the smell of death. Although I couldn't quite identify it at first, I suddenly began to realize what it was and where it was coming from.

I jumped out of bed to locate the corpse. I knew where it was. After all, I should, for I was responsible for it, and knew it had to be moved if I was to get any sleep that night.

I turned on the light, went over to the window, pulled back the curtains and there it was. It was hanging limp, leaning awkwardly against the window-pane. Its natural color had drained out of it, and it had turned a deathly shade of yellow. The cause of its premature demise would have baffled all the experts, but a thorough postmortem would certainly have found that it had died of acute alcoholic poisoning!

Any self-respecting pathologist north of the border would have been horrified to discover that the solution responsible for its death was a tumbler-sized dose of pure malt whisky, Smith's Glenlivet, a 100 per cent proof.

I opened the window to remove the stench, deposited the carcass in the bathroom airing cupboard, and returned to bed. Sleep, however, eluded me; the sudden confrontation with death triggered off an unsolicited meditation on the shortness of life in general, and the shortness of my own life in particular.

An old professor of mine once said that a man hardly thinks of death before he's forty, and hardly thinks of anything else after.

What was the point of it all? What had I achieved? Here was I, a priest, approaching what seemed to me then the beginning of the end, and I had done nothing, got nowhere, and even the man I respected most in the world had hinted that I was hardly out of my spiritual rompers.

Peter sat waiting for us as Father James and I rushed into the tiny departure lounge to check in, when most of the passengers were aboard. The tiny red lights were already beginning to flash on the plane as the engines were revving up for take-off. The sun had still not risen when Peter came out to the steps of the small Island plane with Father James for the final farewells.

"A small thank you for all you've done for me," said Peter, as he thrust a parcel into my hands. "You've saved me hours addressing the letters that would have kept me busy till early autumn. It's a little something I was given in London to keep me warm in the winter, but it's not really my cup of tea," he said smiling.

"Cup of tea, indeed," said Father James. His eyes nearly popped out of his head as the paper wrapper fell off revealing a liter-size bottle of pure malt whisky. "Smith's Glenlivet," '100 per cent proof.'

A change of expression on the face of Father James suddenly alerted me, and I turned quickly and began to make my way up the gangway. Then in a parody of some hack repertory actor, I heard his voice rising up behind me.

"Oh, how sweet a thing is death."

I swept imperiously round, unable to restrain the smile of recognition that spread all over my face, and I replied, "As Shelley said to the Muse."

"No," came the reply. "As the geranium said to the airing cupboard."

I turned as pink as a salmon, as I slithered into my seat.

Peter looked nonplussed as the plane paddled along the foreshore ready for take-off.

I looked down towards Calvay as the plane banked up in the ascent, and I could see Peter's little boat silhouetted against the dramatic red and orange skyline that heralded the early morning sunrise. As the sun rose I could see a single solitary trawler making its way towards the North. It looked innocent enough, but who could tell!

Once again the thoughts of death and the shortness of life that had tormented me the night before flashed into my mind, but this time I brushed them aside. I will begin again, I said to myself. I will begin anew, no matter how many times I may fail. **In the**

Trying is the Dying, and in the Dying is the Rising, Peter had said. So be it. Time may be short, shorter than I might think, but I was going to use every moment left to me now. I wanted to have at least some pride left when I went to meet my Maker.

Little did I know then that the next stage of my spiritual journey would kick the hell out of my pride to let a little bit of heaven in. But that's yet another story, a very long and painful story because it's the story of how a proud and arrogant man has to learn how to try GENTLY and that's the work of a lifetime, that is if you happen to be particularly quick at learning.